The Amish Schools
of Indiana

The Amish Schools of Indiana

Faith in Education

STEPHEN BOWERS HARROFF

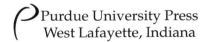

Purdue University Press
West Lafayette, Indiana

Library of Congress Cataloging-in-Publication Data

Harroff, Stephen Bowers, 1942–
   The Amish schools of Indiana : Faith in education / Stephen Bowers Harroff.
      p. cm.
Includes bibliographical references and index.
   ISBN 1-55753-293-1 (hardcover)
1. Amish—Education—Indiana—History. I. Title.

LC586.A45.H37 2003
271.071'7772—dc22

                                          2003021754

Contents

Preface

I have been preparing to write this book since my childhood. When I was in my early teens, my maternal grandfather, Harvey Bowers, after retiring as a math teacher at Wakarusa High School, taught for several years in one of the first Amish parochial schools in Indiana. That school has crossed the path of my own life regularly since my childhood. Most recently, I was privileged to spend some time observing its two hardworking and talented teachers. There I was also privileged to renew a friendship with several of my grandfather's former pupils who regaled me with tales about his history lessons, which were always based upon his travels to the annual conference of our church, the Pietist and Anabaptist Church of the Brethren, in which he was a minister.

Part of my interest in Amish schools thus derives naturally enough from family history. But several other long-term interests of mine also led me to this study. One of these is the pervasive influence of German culture on the history of the United States, and more specifically on Indiana. I have taught German studies for over thirty years now at Indiana University Purdue University Fort Wayne (IPFW) in the midst of northeastern Indiana and the Amish community that forms the third largest settlement area by state, following Ohio and Pennsylvania. One of the issues that came up as I wrote my first article on Amish belief and practice, in 1978, was how Amish teachers and parents might strengthen their children's understanding of the German Bible of Luther, which they use for reading, prayer, and church services.

Another part of my work at IPFW is a course in anthropology that I developed over twenty years ago on the Old Order Amish and Old German Baptist Brethren. My teaching in German studies and in anthropology is combined here with equally strong interests in applied pedagogy and lifelong learning. The Amish have taught me many lessons in this area, for they live a life that does not allow for artificial distinctions between faith and life, between belief and practice, between knowledge and application of knowledge.

My own study of Indiana Amish schools must be viewed in the context of the path-making studies of John Hostetler and Elizabeth Enders Huntington, whose book *Amish Children* set the standard for all subsequent studies of Amish children in school. I have used their books and articles in my anthropology course for over twenty years now, and I know that my students would want me to honor their work here. I have also met them in person at professional meetings, and I can say that they each exemplify the German phrase *Nun, das ist ein Mensch!* They have been kind, unassuming, and helpful to colleagues and students, friends and acquaintances. While this book was reaching its final revisions, John A. Hostetler died in Goshen, Indiana. His wise and gentle scholarly manner will be greatly missed.

I especially would like to thank the many Amish teachers, pupils, parents, and school board members who helped make this study possible by naming them here, but that is not the Amish way. I hope that they will recognize themselves in my descriptions and that they will enjoy their own personal copy of my study. My deeply felt thanks to L. and to A.; to my dear friends D. and D., I owe a very special thank you, for you have taught me by your own example and you have refreshed my spirit.

I would also like to thank my friend and colleague Chad Thompson, associate professor of English, linguistics, and anthropology, for his years of attention to my work, for the delightful and very helpful discussions that we have had as I worked on this project, and for what I have learned from his strong research program with the Old Order Amish of Indiana.

I have learned to rely on and treasure my talks with Margaret Hunt, managing editor of the Purdue University Press, whose keen insights on the enterprise of publishing and on education are teamed with a strong background in German studies. And Jennifer Tyrrell, my editor at Purdue Press, has been an enthusiastic, energetic questioner of my every observation—always with the reader in mind. Her suggestions for moving paragraphs from one place to another and for amplifying other passages have made this book more readable and enjoyable.

Finally, I would like to thank my wife, Susan, for her steadfast belief in my work, for the ideas that we have shared, and for her reading of every word of this manuscript. She has been the first editor for every study that I have published. I cannot find words to express my gratitude to her and my admiration for how she lives her life.

Although all names of persons and references to schools have been changed in an attempt to preserve anonymity, the descriptions are as accurate as I could make them. When I was observing in a school, I took copious notes preserving as much as possible the exact wording of both teacher and pupil. My interviews with parents and school board members also involved pages of hand-written notes. In deference to Amish practice, I did not make any tape recordings. I have tried very hard to be fair and accurate in my descriptions and in my discussion, but I also know that perfection lies beyond the human plane. All mistakes in this book are my own.

The Amish Schools
of Indiana

Introduction
The Substitute

<hr>

It is very early on a Wednesday morning as I arrive at school. The pupils will begin arriving at 7:25 A.M., but Teacher Steve arrives by 6:45. There is just the faintest glimmer of dawn on the horizon on this late February morning, and the schoolroom is very dark. I fumble around putting away my things, and realize I have forgotten something very important—my flashlight. This means I will have to light the pressurized white-gas lamp, for the first time, with whatever light is coming through the window. I can see the knob for turning on the gas and also the smaller knob up higher, which probably releases the gas into the twin mantels for lighting. But what is that other lever that looks like it could be set either up or down? *Ach!* No matter—the teacher for whom I am substituting probably set it exactly where it belongs before we left school the day before. Good! Turn on the lower knob; turn on the upper knob; listen for the hiss; strike a match near the mantels; and, presto, the mantels explode with light. Whoa! What's this? Flaming gas is cascading down the long wooden pole of the lamp assembly heading right toward the gas bottle below! *Ach!* I put my hands over the flames to keep them from the bottle and quickly shut off the lower knob—even teachers can do dumb things. Thank goodness, gross darkness again covers my part of the earth.

My hands hurt. I am a *college* professor, weak from too much contemplating, and I am not Amish, so how could I have thought I could be an adequate substitute! My Anabaptist and Pietist heritage

1

made me want to. All right, Stephen, get a grip; you have thirty years of teaching experience, and fifty-four years of life experience. At least you didn't explode the tank and burn down the school on your first day as a substitute! Be thankful!

It is now nearly 7:00, and I still have much to do—in the dark. At least I know how to shake down ashes and rekindle the fire in the coal stove. It takes about five minutes to do that task and to adjust the draft and crack a window or two for fresh air. As I am finishing, the middle-grade teacher arrives. She gives me a friendly, "Hi, Steve," and then adds immediately, "Why are you working in the dark?" I explain my near disaster to her with real contrition. She laughs heartily and says, "See that little petcock up there? (I had noticed it, *ja.*) When it's down, it puts out too much gas; just turn it up, and it'll work fine. Like this." She certainly knows how to light up my life this morning, my competent, cheerful, helpful friend—she is also an excellent teacher.

7:10. My pupils will be arriving in fifteen minutes, and I still have to put the assignments in arithmetic for the sixth, seventh, and eighth grades on the board and write out a problem for each class. And I also want to put up my thought for the day that I read in the monthly periodical for Amish schoolteachers: "It is easier to do a job right than to explain why you didn't" (*Blackboard Bulletin*, May 1994, 9). How will I feel about that one when I see my friend after he returns?

The busses arrive just as I am finishing my board work and sitting down at the desk for a quick sip of coffee from my thermos. The morning hours go very well, and I am beginning to feel proud of myself: "Pride goeth before destruction and an haughty spirit before a fall." Then comes noon recess. I hear scuffling and noise from the cloakroom, and then a group of older boys breaks out, one of whom is wearing a girl's *Kapp,* a white prayer covering that girls wear all day at school, removing it only in private to rearrange their hair if it gets unruly. No boy should be wearing a prayer covering! And no girl would want to be without hers! I give the boys a hard look and say, "Give it back to her." They do so right away. As they go outside to play, I feel proud of myself again, for I am not used to giving discipline in my college classes, and I am not well known for my hard looks.

I hear doors slamming and footsteps running on the lower level of the school. I am writing some important notes on the board for the afternoon classes, and since the noise soon stops, I continue working. Pretty soon my friend, the other teacher, comes into my room and says, "Your boys were running all over the school and slamming doors. I asked them if they would be allowed to do such a thing at home. Then I told them that they should think of this school as their home and treat it respectfully." What made my ears get red was her passing reference to "my" boys. I forgot that important role of teacher as parent figure. Her words to the boys were just the right touch—but they should have come from me. School is full of lessons for everyone, including Teacher Steve. And I know there will be more before we go home.

I have never had to give grades for deportment, and I certainly don't want to do so in my friend's classroom. After all, I am just a substitute. But now, at the end of the day, while everyone is working hard on their reading homework, and I am answering questions for several seventh graders, a spit wad lands right in front of me on my desk. It bounces in such a way that I can guess its trajectory, from the near right, from the eighth-grade boys. I look up and give a hard look, but I also know that isn't enough. "Remember, less is more," I tell myself, and so I simply say, "It looks as though someone is working for a low deportment grade." After I dismiss the class to go to the busses, several eighth-grade boys rush up to my desk and want to see their deportment grade. I say I haven't given any—today—but that I would certainly have to think hard about doing so again tomorrow unless things went better. The next day was nearly idyllic.

Several weeks later, I was asked to substitute again, at the last moment, for the first- and second-grade teacher. This was a large classroom with nearly thirty pupils. The teacher had left me instructions for what subjects to teach, and I had spent a week in her room observing and had seen teachers at other Amish schools work with these two grades. Moreover, I knew many of the children in this classroom by reference to their older brothers and sisters and by having seen them on the playground nearly every day during the winter months. And one final clincher for me was the fact that my mother had been a second-grade teacher for many years, so I said I would be glad to substitute for the younger children.

The teaching was very enjoyable. What I had forgotten was that first graders particularly want to confirm everything they do with Teacher. No matter what the activity, from their homework in *More Numbers with Spunky the Donkey*, to their reading workbooks, to their seatwork books, virtually every first grader had a question for Teacher Steve. Some wanted reassurance that their answer was correct before they went on to the next problem—every time; some had procedural questions, "May I do the next page, too?"; some wanted my opinion as an artist, "Is this color good for a robin?"; some merely wanted to be noticed by the teacher. It all took an incredible amount of time. They were always very quiet and polite, and if I was helping another pupil, they would sit until I got to them. But by 10:00 A.M. nearly every first-grade hand was in the air, and I still had to work with the second grade. Then an angel of mercy appeared in the guise of an Amish mother—Martha, the wife of the chairman of the school board—who asked if she could give me a hand. I later found out that my friend the third- through fifth-grade teacher had been listening in as she taught and had sent one of her fourth graders home with the message: "Steve needs some help." So I guess I would have to say that there were two angels of mercy involved. Martha took over the first-grade questioners while I went on to the second grade. She stayed until after 1:00 P.M., but then *apologized* for having to leave early to begin preparations for dinner for her family! She had saved the day, but within the hour the first-grade questions had started again. They all wanted to finish their homework before the busses came at 2:30, which was a worthy goal. I thought it might help if I stayed at my desk and had them come to me. It worked . . . until about 2:20, when I saw the first bus pull in. I still had six first graders lined up at my desk with questions! I knew I had to stand up and say, "Put away your books," or the children would be left behind. So I began to walk to the door to dismiss the children, and all six first graders followed me like ducklings in a line all the way to the back of the room—in perfect rank order, first questioner to sixth questioner! What a parade! I felt like, and probably looked like, Mother Goose.

I only substituted three times that semester, but I thoroughly enjoyed it. I learned a lot about myself as a teacher and as a person. And I also learned that teachers in Amish schools work as hard as Amish carpenters and Amish mothers. The sheer amount of energy necessary to keep three classes going is astonishing: one class must be taught actively; another class must be finishing a homework assignment from the day before in preparation for grading; and the third must be working on the current homework assignment. The cadence that one falls into after a few hours of this work certainly helps, but the teacher must balance these activities, watch for the hands of pupils who have questions, and keep an eye out for anyone who needs a hard stare.

Order is very important to the Old Order Amish, and I can see now that an orderly approach to the work of the school day is essential. It is certainly also true that Amish children are so well behaved that teaching can progress easily. They know that this is their job, that they are expected to work hard and consistently, and that they are to mind the teacher. They also know that the family support system will find out quickly if they misbehave, and they know that Mom and Dad take their job of parenting very seriously, too.

The Old Order Amish parochial schools in Indiana are growing strongly, but what is it like to teach in or attend an Amish school in Indiana at the beginning of the twenty-first century? We will explore this topic and the ways contemporary Amish culture interprets the Anabaptist belief system as we seek to uncover reasons for the success of these schools.

Chapter One
Indiana Amish Schools: 1948–2002

Religion, morality, and knowledge being necessary to good
government and the happiness of mankind, schools, and
the means of education shall forever be encouraged.
—Northwest Ordinance of 1787, Article 3
United States Congress[1]

When Jeffersonian democracy began to spread westward in these
United States, the new Northwest Territory (what is now Ohio,
Indiana, Michigan, Illinois, and Wisconsin) needed a charter that
would direct the lives of those who would first settle this densely
forested wilderness. As children of the Enlightenment, our forefathers believed that education was the most fundamental enterprise
of freedom, that an educated citizenry would see to the needs of the
state, and that one of the first tasks of a new settlement was to provide schooling for the next generation. And so one-room schools in
Indiana began. Scholars estimate that as recently as 1913 there were
212,000 one-room schools in the United States, enrolling 50 percent
of American schoolchildren.[2]

This would all change in the ensuing forty years as the nation experienced two horrendous world wars and the joblessness and
bread lines of the Great Depression. Somewhere in that dark period,

we learned that factories provided efficiencies of scale and breadth of product that we could admire. The businessmen who were also our congressmen in state government began to apply these lessons to our schools, creating factories for learning. The goal of creating an educated citizenry became the process of mass education.

In Indiana, state representatives pushed for consolidation of country schools based upon economic considerations, upon the greater breadth of subject matter that large schools could offer, and upon the competitive environment that such schools would automatically provide. Amish and non-Amish families found their communities disrupted by school consolidation. During the forties and fifties, Indiana one-room schools, like those in Wakarusa and Nappanee, could no longer remain small, local, community, and township-based schools. Instead, economic and political forces of the modern world determined that they consolidate, and schools like Wa-Nee, named for *Wakarusa* and *Nappanee*, were opened. Thus, school consolidation in Indiana has led to huge school systems, often named *corporations* using the factory/business model, with huge budgets and huge administrative costs. They are a reflection of modern life.

The Old Order Amish reject modernism. They do so in part because of the excesses and prideful lifestyles of modern life and in part because they perceive in modern life a fragmentation of the family and its values. In his noted work *The Riddle of Amish Culture*, Donald Kraybill asserts, " . . . only by shunning modernity have [the Amish] been able to survive."[3] When the local country schools in Indiana, operated by township boards in which Amish parents had participated, were closed during the late forties, Amish parents learned that their children would be transported many miles from home and would be taught in large, complex buildings in a setting where they knew neither teachers nor classmates. Indiana Amish communities, like their counterparts in Pennsylvania and Ohio, soon established their own parochial schools.

In 1948, when I was just entering school, the first Amish parochial school opened in the Elkhart-LaGrange settlement, then and now the largest contiguous community of Old Order Amish in Indiana. The building, a one-room county school that had been closed the previous year due to consolidation, was purchased at auction by the Amish for $3,225 and renamed Plain View School.[4] Total enrollment in grades one through eight that first year was twenty-nine pupils.

Two years later in 1951, the Nappanee settlement opened the Borkholder School, the second Amish parochial school in Indiana, and the one in which my maternal grandfather taught. It had also been a one-room county public school. It was closed and then returned to the estate of the Borkholder family, which had originally donated the land on which the school was built. The family then turned the school over to the Amish school committee, and the Borkholder School opened as an Amish parochial school with an enrollment of forty-two students in grades one through nine.[5] By the end of the fifties, as consolidation was becoming widespread, four small Amish parochial schools had opened in Indiana, two in the Elkhart-LaGrange settlement, and one each in the Allen County and Nappanee settlements.

By the end of the sixties, public school consolidation had been accomplished in Indiana. Thus, the Amish parochial school movement in Indiana coincided with the progression of school consolidation. This linkage is not peculiar to Indiana and the Amish school movement here. What is significant and uncommon is that the early development of Amish parochial schools in Indiana followed a peaceful and progressive path, due largely to the cooperation of Richard Wells, superintendent of public instruction in Indiana, with the Amish School Committee. The decade of the sixties saw the official acceptance of the Amish parochial school plan by the state of Indiana. In August 1967, the Amish School Committee (currently ten men from the five major settlements[6]) met with Indiana Superintendent of Public Instruction Wells and published a set of articles of agreement, which came to be known in public school circles as the Wells Agreement.[7] This agreement is still used today; indeed, at a regional school meeting that I attended in 1997, the updated version of it was handed out to each school by a member of the Amish State School Board—a group which had its beginning with that agreement. The agreement, now titled *Regulations and Guidelines for Amish Parochial Schools of Indiana,* is occasionally revised by the Amish members of their state school board, chaired by a man from the Elkhart-LaGrange settlement, and reprinted by an Amish publisher in Pennsylvania.[8] It specifies the minimum number of days the Amish parochial schools must be in session (167), the minimum average attendance rate on those days (97 percent), general guidelines for the curriculum, the need to meet guidelines of the state fire marshal in new school construction, general guidelines for school boards, and the establishment of a state school board for the Amish parochial schools.

Given this official recognition of the Amish right to establish their own parochial schools, it is no wonder that the decade of the sixties saw a tenfold increase in the number of schools. By the end of that decade there were 42 Amish schools, 20 in the Elkhart-LaGrange settlement, 8 in the Nappanee settlement, 6 in the Daviess County settlement, 7 in the Adams County settlement, 3 in the Allen County settlement, and 1 in the Kokomo settlement.

Another highly significant influence on the rapid growth of the Amish parochial schools in Indiana, and virtually everywhere that Amish reside, was the 1972 United States Supreme Court decision in *Wisconsin* v. *Yoder* which permits Amish children of age fifteen to complete their formal schooling with the eighth grade.[9] Prior to this time, a section of the *Regulations and Guidelines* allowed children younger than sixteen to complete their formal schooling in an apprenticeship program that had them work under the supervision of an Amish adult and complete written assignments once a week about this work. Since 1972, the apprenticeship program has been discontinued in Indiana Amish parochial schools. Thus, the decade of the seventies brought yet another landmark agreement that would have a strongly positive effect on the growth of the Indiana Amish parochial schools for several decades. In the seventies, the number of Amish schools in Indiana reached fifty-four; and by the eighties, the number was seventy-one.

Public school consolidation in the fifties, the agreement with the Indiana superintendent of public instruction in the late sixties, and the landmark Supreme Court decision in the early seventies provided significant external impetuses to the growth of Amish parochial schools in Indiana. But there are also important internal factors that support the growth of these schools, and these factors become particularly relevant for the growth spurt during the nineties.

First, each Amish parochial school is a community school; the school building is the only building that the Amish church district supports, since they meet for worship in members' homes rather than in a church building. The school is built on land donated by an Amish family; it is built by members of the church district in which it is located; and it is maintained by them both physically and financially. Amish parents pay property taxes like all other citizens, and must then support their own schools in addition. This requires considerable sacrifice of time and wealth, and significant planning as well, but provides them the opportunity to ensure their children are being exposed to the ideals of their society continuously. Although it is the local Amish school board that hires the teachers and oversees the curriculum and general activities at the school, the head teacher at the school and the parents of its students have a strong influence on their decisions.

Second, learning in the Amish parochial school reflects the Anabaptist heritage and belief system in ways that would be impossible in public schools. Each day begins with prayer and usually with a period of singing hymns or listening to religious materials read aloud by the teacher.[10] Lunch also begins and ends with prayer. The school uniform is the Amish clothing that these children wear as part of their religious heritage. Teachers are responsible for creating a learning environment that reflects Amish values as expressed in the community. Learning occurs in a quiet, respectful, orderly atmosphere. Pupils are taught that learning is work and that good work is expected of every Amish Christian as a biblical imperative. Teachers do not lavish praise on their pupils because that does not comport with Amish views on self-aggrandizement. Amish teachers say, "Yes" or "Correct," rather than "Good" or "Great."

Third, the curriculum and the curricular materials of Amish parochial schools reflect Amish interests very well. Amish parents want their children to have strong arithmetic skills that they can apply in their work after they leave school. This means that boys must be able to apply geometry and algebra directly as they build and calculate; girls must be able to maintain checking, saving, and even investment accounts, work with financial planning and record keeping in their home industry—a particular emphasis in recent years in Indiana—and they must be able to use arithmetic procedures to plan large meals. Strong English writing, reading, and vocabulary skills are also expected of all pupils, for English literacy is a requisite part of life in the United States. Amish schools in Indiana focus on phonics from first grade often into the upper grades, and now also teach German reading for understanding in the context of the Bible translation by Luther and other curricular materials derived directly from Scripture. Other subjects such as history, geography, health, or general science also play a role, but it is clear that reading, writing, and arithmetic are the mainstay of the Amish school curriculum.

This is not a diluted approach to education. It is understood in the Indiana Amish community that one must learn to read, write, and figure as part of one's faith which considers the body to be the temple of the spirit. Amish schools prepare pupils to be strong, productive, self-regulating, faithful members of the Amish community. Their success in this enterprise clearly is reflected in the continuing growth of their schools.

As of this writing, in the spring of 2001, there are more than 5,100 pupils enrolled in more than 135 Amish parochial schools in Indiana. The Amish schools vary rather significantly in the number of children enrolled per school. One Amish settlement (Allen County) prefers larger schools, often with four classrooms; they enroll slightly more than one hundred pupils per school. Other settlements build smaller schools with two classrooms, and these schools more typically enroll forty to fifty pupils. The "2000–2001 School Directory" printed by the Amish in *Blackboard Bulletin* shows Indi-

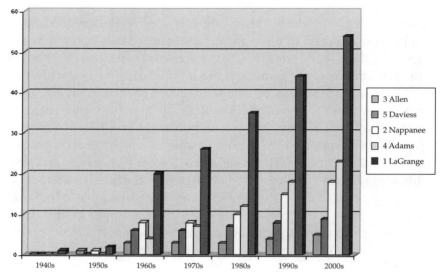

Chart 1.1

ana Amish parochial schools have an average enrollment of 37.8 pupils per school, and 18.2 pupils per teacher.[11]

One important measure of the growth of Old Order Amish parochial schools in Indiana is the growth in the *number of schools* each decade since the fifties in the five largest Indiana Amish settlement areas. Chart 1.1 demonstrates graphically how robust the growth has been. The growth rate continues despite current building costs, instructional costs, and availability of teachers. Reasons for the growth are both external (public school consolidation; official acceptance of Amish schools by the state; 1972 Supreme Court decision) and internal (school as only community-owned building; integration of Anabaptist heritage and values into both daily schedule and curriculum).

To understand why settlements support several schools simultaneously it is important to compare the total number of *schools* with the number of *Amish church districts*. This comparison is best illustrated in chart 1.2 by looking at each of the five largest settlements to get a sense of the relative geographic proximity to one's school that these settlements reach towards. These two graphs (charts 1.1

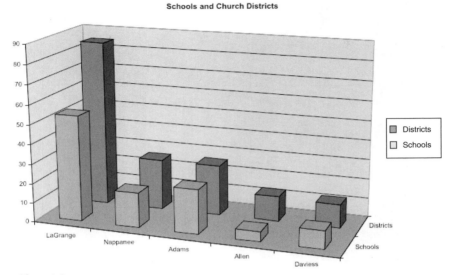

Chart 1.2

and 1.2) address the Amish interest in keeping their children in small, truly local schools—the issue that led them to begin building their schools in the late forties and the fifties.

We can see this growth in the Plain View School and Borkholder School. Plain View School, the first Amish parochial school, opened in 1948; the total enrollment in grades one through eight that first year was twenty-nine pupils. In 2000–01, Plain View, recently remodeled (plate 1.1), enrolled nearly the same number of pupils (31), but it has been joined by fifty-three additional schools in that settlement alone, and the combined reported enrollment of these fifty-four schools is now 1,802 pupils.[12]

Borkholder School, too, is still open, although the original building was replaced in 2000 by a new structure (plate 1.2); it had an enrollment of 29 pupils in grades one through eight for 2000–01, but it had been joined by seventeen other Amish parochial schools in that settlement, enrolling some 586 pupils.[13] Until the 2000–01 school year, the original Borkholder School building (plates 1.3 and 1.4) was the oldest one-room school in Indiana still in operation, having enrolled pupils for over one hundred years.[14]

1.1 Plain View School: the oldest school in Indiana, founded in 1948 and remodeled in 2000.

1.2 Borkholder School: the second Amish parochial school in Indiana, founded in 1954, remodeled several times, and finally completely rebuilt in 2000.

1.3 **Original Borkholder School:** at one time the oldest one-room school in Indiana since it had been a county school before being deeded over to the Amish during school consolidation.

1.4 **Original Borkholder School (Inside View):** a German lesson is on the blackboard and pussy willows bring a touch of nature's beauty into this classroom, where my maternal grandfather taught when I was a child.

Another important measure of growth in Indiana Amish schools is the *total enrollment* in the schools. At the end of the fifties, there were 60 pupils enrolled at Plain View, 29 at Pleasant Ridge (both in the Elkhart-LaGrange settlement),[15] 51 pupils in the Borkholder School near the Nappanee settlement,[16] and an estimated 15 at Amish Parochial #1 in the Allen County settlement, which enrolled only seventh and eighth grades at that time.[17] The estimated total at the end of the fifties would thus be slightly more than 150 pupils in the four Amish parochial schools. During the 2000–01 school year, the Amish schools reported enrollment of 5,106 pupils in 135 schools with 280 teachers.[18]

If we compare the enrollment of the consolidated public schools with that of the Amish parochial schools then and now, we can get a stronger sense of the effects of this movement. Small country schools in Shipshewana, LaGrange, Middlebury, Topeka, Wolcottville and Rome City were closed and the rural consolidation Westview was opened in 1967,[19] and in 2002, Westview's average enrollment per elementary school was 376. The thirty-four Amish parochial schools in the coverage area of this district reported enrollments that averaged thirty-nine students for the same period.[20] In Adams County the picture is similar, except that here the Amish settlement is split between two public school consolidations, Adams Central and South Adams. The Adams Central 2002 average enrollment per elementary/middle school was 432 pupils; the ten Amish parochial schools in this district reported enrollments averaging 49 pupils for 2002 (one school had no report). The South Adams 2002 average enrollment per elementary/middle school was 429 pupils, and the fourteen Amish schools in this district reported an average enrollment of 41 (one school not reporting).[21] The rural consolidation East Allen County Schools (EACS) was formed by closing small country schools in and around Leo, Grabill, Harlan, Woodburn, Monroeville, Hoagland, and New Haven. In 2002, the average enrollment per EACS elementary/middle school was 466 students while the six largest Amish parochial schools in this coverage area reported average enrollments of 107 (one school did not report figures).[22] This list of consolidated schools accounts only for those areas of Northern Indiana that are home to the majority of Indiana's Old Order Amish

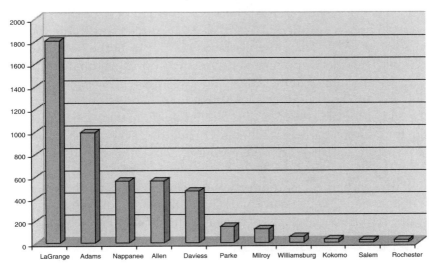

Chart 1.3

families: the Elkhart-LaGrange, Nappanee, Adams County and Allen County settlements. If one considers only the five consolidated school districts described above (Wa-Nee, Westview, Adams Central, South Adams, and East Allen County) the average consolidated school enrolls 453 pupils. The Amish schools in these same five areas of Northern Indiana reported an average school enrollment of fifty-three in the same period, or *12 percent the size* of the average consolidated elementary and middle school.

The third chart (chart 1.3) graphs the *total number of pupils* enrolled in Amish schools by settlement area for the 2000–01 school year and includes all settlements in the state. Data are missing from fifteen of the schools: 2 schools in the Bennington settlement; 3 schools in the Elkhart-LaGrange settlement; 5 schools in the Orange County settlement; 3 schools in the Steuben County settlement; 1 school in the Whitley County settlement; and 1 school in the Worthington settlement. (For purposes of keeping their data, the Amish authors of the yearly report in *Blackboard Bulletin* assume that schools sending no report have one teacher and twenty pupils.) The

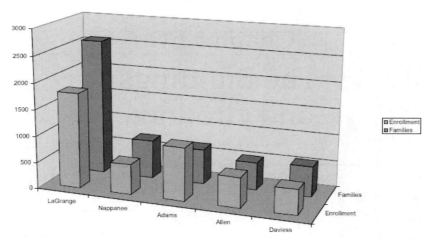

Chart 1.4

chart makes clear that five settlements account for most of the Amish parochial school enrollments in the state: Elkhart-LaGrange, Nappanee, Adams County, Allen County, and Daviess County. Their percentage of the total reported enrollment in 2000–01 is 91 percent (4444 of 4870); if one uses the total *estimated* enrollment, which includes the nonreporting schools as well, the percentage of the five largest settlements is 88 percent (4499 of 5106).

The final chart (chart 1.4) describes the five largest settlements by graphing the *enrollment* in the Amish parochial schools with the *number of families* in each settlement. This gives one measure of the relative support for these schools within the settlement. You will note that the enrollment in the Adams County settlement actually exceeds the number of families in the settlement, a measure that is not typical of the other four settlements. This may be accounted for by the fact that many Adams County Amish families are very large.

Most references to schools in this text will focus on these five settlements, with particular reference to seven schools that I have studied more extensively. These schools show typical variations of age, physical size, enrollment, and grouping of classes for which a teacher is responsible.

Chapter Two
The Buildings and Grounds

The variation of design and size of the Old Order Amish parochial schools in Indiana is often settlement specific, just as issues of clothing, transportation, and even work are determined by the *Ordnung* of church districts within the specific settlements. This set of unwritten principles of church membership, reaffirmed by all church members once a year, determines, for example, that Allen County Amish drive open buggies the year round and that LaGrange County Amish always drive closed buggies.[1] Large settlements, like those mentioned above, have multiple church districts. Each of these districts has its own Ordnung, which comports, not always completely but mostly, with the other Ordnungen in the settlement. Therefore, due to the Ordnungen, the Amish parochial schools within a settlement have very similar designs and functions.

We will begin our discussion with what all of the Indiana Amish parochial schools have in common; this includes the rural setting of the school and the school grounds. Of primary concern to the Indiana Amish who started the parochial school movement was the small, rural nature of the school setting. In fact, one Amish source clearly states that there would have been no need for the Amish to begin their own parochial schools if the one-room country school movement had continued.[2]

2.1 Allen County One-Room Public School (1930s): from the holdings of the Allen County Public Library. The Amish girl in the center is the great grandmother of a family featured in this book.

Thus, their initial impetus was not at all to separate themselves from their country neighbors with whom they had been schooled since the first schools were established in Indiana. Plate 2.1, from the holdings of the Allen County Public Library, shows the pupils of a country public school in eastern Allen County during the thirties. In the midst of the old school photo are Old Order Amish children whose descendents still live in Allen County. All Amish children attended *public* schools in Indiana before school consolidation began.

Contemporary Amish parochial schools in Indiana are always found in a traditional, albeit changing, rural setting. They are located on country roads. Some of these roads are paved, particularly in the Elkhart-LaGrange settlement, while most others are dirt roads. These country roads have a vista that is in tune with nature and not dominated by human-made objects. Virtually all school plots were

2.2 Summer Break at an Elkhart-LaGrange Amish Parochial School:
virtually all schools are fenced in with a stock gate at the entrance and have
no landscaping or plantings, so that sheep (or horses, or cattle) can graze
there during the summer months.

originally a section of some working Amish farm that still surrounds the school. Some schools are still part of fields that are used
as pasture during the summer months when school is not in session.
Plate 2.2 shows sheep grazing in the schoolyard of an Elkhart-
LaGrange Amish school. Here, one can still see the horizon. There
are no factory-like buildings to break up one's view of nature. The
largest buildings nearby are usually barns. One sees open, cultivat-
ed fields and animals grazing in pastures and woods. Some Amish
schools put out bluebird houses on the fence posts surrounding the
school so that the children may experience springtime delight in the
birth of one of God's most beautiful creatures.

From the windows of an Indiana Amish school, children see
barns, draft horses, driving horses, and cows in pastures rimmed
by woods. They see corn being planted in spring and harvested in

2.3 Recess at a Daviess County Amish School: a softball game is always a favorite; and the teacher often gets to pitch.

2.4 Older Amish Schoolchildren at Recess: While older children play volleyball, the younger pupils play on the swings, teeter totter, or slide, if they have one.

the late fall. They can watch the winter wheat begin to grow again in early spring. They learn in a setting that they know well because it is part of the farm of a church member from their district or one immediately adjacent to their own. What they hear when the windows are open—as they usually are—is the sound of cattle lowing, an occasional whinny, bird calling, the clopping of horse hooves as a buggy passes by the school, and once in a very great while, the sudden blasting of a boat horn from a buggy driven by a young man who graduated from school to full-time work a year or two before.

The grounds of the school are not landscaped with shrubs and flowers but are kept both plain and simple, in keeping with the Amish practice of *Demut* (humility), so that they can be used for summer grazing of livestock. The grounds always include an open yard, which is used during recess for such group activities as freeze tag, fox and geese, and even running contests. Most schools also have a ball diamond with a backstop, bases, and a pitching mound. One of the favorite activities at noon is a softball game played by teacher and pupils (plate 2.3), and the end-of-school ball game between the fathers and the schoolchildren is played with great enthusiasm and some huffing and puffing. At some schools the ball diamond is also used for such contests on Saturdays during the summer months. Indiana Amish schools also have at least one volleyball court and a typical swing set and teeter-totter for the younger children (plate 2.4). Most also have a basketball court, in some instances paved, and a tetherball pole.

Virtually all schools have a small barn or shed for the horses of teachers and pupils who come to school in a buggy (plate 2.5). Outbuildings also house a supply of coal or wood for heating in the winter. Some schools have a pump house, occasionally with a motor for pressurizing a tank. At least two schools have recently added photocopy machines that are operated with large battery packs and/or inverters. Many schools continue to use Spirit Master machines, but I assume that more schools will adopt the photocopy machine if their Ordnung changes to allow it. Nearly every school has at least one outhouse (plate 2.6); a few have indoor plumbing.

2.5 School Barn: all schools have a shed or small barn to house the horses of teachers and pupils.

2.6 The Outhouse: some schools have one outhouse; others have two; and one Allen County school has an indoor facility.

2.7 Lighting by Gas Lamp and Large Windows: Allen County Amish use pressurized-gas lamps with mantles in their homes and schools.

2.8 School Mailbox in LaGrange County: although uncommon, this decorative outdoor reminder of the school name says "welcome."

All schools have many large windows to catch available sunlight so that school can be conducted as much as possible using natural lighting. In winter, schools use the same kind of lighting found in homes in that settlement (plate 2.7).

All Indiana Amish parochial schools have names, many of them with great local flavor and some humor (Plain View, Little Acorn,

Pumpkinvine, Eight Square, Hawpatch, Swiss Valley, and Coyote Hollow). It is rare for a school to have a nameplate affixed to it; very few even have the name of the school on the mailbox, this is in keeping with Anabaptist teachings on pride and open display of anything but a business name (plate 2.8). Inside the school, where it is less proud or worldly, the school name is often placed on a poster welcoming visitors, particularly parents, to the school.

The type of school building used is determined by the Ordnungen of each Amish settlement, and so these will be described by settlement so that we can see the context in which learning takes place in the Amish parochial schools, with a focus on the five largest: Elkhart-LaGrange, Nappanee, Adams County, Allen County and Daviess County. Only the Allen County Amish build schools with more than two rooms; and the four newest of their six schools are of brick rather than sided frame construction. We will begin with them.

Each of the six Allen County Amish parochial school buildings can house more than one hundred pupils. This is virtually twice the number of pupils per school as in the other settlements. Amish children in Allen County are bussed to school, and this transportation means may account for the larger size of their schools. During the 2000–01 school year the public school system delivered Amish children before picking up and delivering children to the public school. This has caused a change in the Amish school schedule so that they now convene approximately one hour earlier than in previous years, at 7:30 A.M.

The oldest Amish school in the Allen County settlement comprises two buildings several hundred yards apart on one plot of land. The original school building, built in 1959, is a story-and-a-half structure with a front entranceway and stairwell, a full basement, and a rear extension for a small library and storage. The building has two large classrooms, one housing forty-one first and second graders in the basement, and another upstairs for thirty-one seventh and eighth graders. The second building is single-story and is also divided into two separate and spacious rooms, housing grades three and four and grades five and six, with an enrollment of

2.9 The Oldest Allen County School: notice the larger rural Amish setting where farmers work their fields (top right) while children work their minds; as this school grew larger, the community added extra buildings in a campus setting.

thirty-five in one room and thirty-four in the other. The total enrollment at this school, between the two buildings, is 169 students.[3] The two buildings are frame construction, and each building has a separate playground. The single-buggy shed is located at the back corner of the property (plate 2.9). All of the Allen County Amish schools use modern coal stoves in each classroom for heating (plate 2.10).

The next oldest Allen County Amish parochial school was built in 1964. It is a multi-level building with a large single-story extension on the front. The inner two-story portion has two classrooms, one upper and one lower, with toilet facilities inside. The extension at the front also has two spacious classrooms. Each of these sections is frame construction. The current enrollment at this school is 127 students (plate 2.11).

2.10 Heating by Coal Stove: Allen County Amish homes and schools use these efficient coal stoves for heat. The aluminum foil radiates heat for warming up sandwiches at noon.

2.11 Allen County Amish Children Arrive at School Early: their school day starts before sunrise much of the year.

2.12 An Allen County School Summer Auction: the fundraiser is an event under the big tent that draws people from all over the wider community.

2.13 Dividers Make Two Classrooms When Closed: or one large
community room for programs or meetings when they are opened.

The newest Allen County Amish schools are brick construction.
The first brick school was built in 1969 as a two-story building. During the nineties, a single-story extension was added to the back of
the building for the upper grades. This school currently enrolls 126
pupils in four classrooms. Behind the buildings is a rather spacious
barn.

The Allen County Amish school built in 1994 (plate 2.12) also has
three classrooms in use; its initial plan included a fourth classroom,
which will be used when needed. Enrollment at this school was
ninety-seven pupils for 2000–01. The school has a single-story extension in the front and an outhouse on one side of the building.
The brick building has two large classrooms on the upper story that
are separated by a series of heavy wooden panels (plate 2.13). Be-
neath these lay the basement classrooms, one of which is used for
the first and second grades while the other currently has a number
of Ping-Pong tables set up for recreation. This room is also used for
carry-in school lunches, which the mothers provide on an occa-

2.14 Drinking Fountains and Washbasins Inside: hygiene is better and easier in this relatively new school; Amish homes in Allen County also now have modern indoor plumbing and cabinetry in their bathrooms and kitchens.

sional basis. This building has several innovations including a ramp for wheelchair access, indoor drinking fountains and washbasins in the entranceway (plate 2.14), and a small library in the front. At one side is a medium-sized barn for the horses, coal storage, and the water pump. The school has cemented basketball courts front and rear, an area for volleyball near the barn, and a large yard for running and ball games. There is also a long cement pad at the back of the property for the buggies of visitors, but most days this area is used for in-line skating at recess.

A fifth Allen County Amish parochial school was added in 1999, enrolling thirty-nine pupils during its first year of operation and forty-six in the 2000–01 school year; due to this increase, a sixth school was needed by the 2001–02 school year. These two schools were built to house a higher pupil enrollment as you can see from plate 2.15. The average enrollment in each of the other four Allen County Amish parochial schools is 130 pupils.

2.15 New Allen County Amish School: the outhouse and buggy shed stand behind the school, while the eighth-grade boys go out for a high, long infield fly—a cold one, if you miss.

All other Amish parochial schools in Indiana are modeled on the old one-room country school, single-story or story-and-a-half with a porch off the front. Most have been built new or remodeled into two-room schools, but their outer appearance maintains the look of the country school of the 1930s. These school buildings are much smaller and more numerous than those in the Allen County settlement, rarely enrolling more than fifty pupils. I will describe one older and one more recent school building in each of the other large settlements.

The Elkhart-LaGrange settlement currently has fifty-four Amish parochial schools with an average enrollment of thirty-five pupils per school. One older school, a one-story cinder block building with a front entranceway, was built in 1965 (plate 2.16). A later frame addition was added to the back. Thus, the school now has two separate classrooms, one of which housed fifteen pupils and the other housed twenty during a recent school year, for a total of thirty-five

2.16 Older Elkhart-LaGrange Amish School: the cinderblock is the oldest—
and best—part of the building according to the head teacher, who finds it
cooler in August and warmer in the winter months.

pupils in grades one through eight. A very small shed serves as a
stable for horses as well as for limited storage.

One school that I visited in 1997 is one of three built in 1995. This
modern building has a full basement with a central furnace and a
classroom on one side that was used for special education pupils
during the 1997–98 school year. A large, open classroom area at
ground level serves the whole school, currently fifty-six pupils, for
many activities and then is divided by a heavy drape so that it can
contain two classrooms when the two teachers do individual work.
Upstairs is a small, modern apartment arranged for cooking and
sleeping, suitable for the three young teachers who have to travel
from the other side of the large settlement to teach here. They return
home for the weekend and stay above the school during the school
week. This arrangement of having very modest living quarters
above the school is common in the Elkhart-LaGrange and Nappanee settlements. A typical apartment has a kitchenette with a small
gas stove and gas refrigerator, modern kitchen cabinetry, stainless

steel double sink, breakfast bar, and two small bedrooms with space for a bed and a dresser.[4] A small shed is used for horses and for storage. This school has a typical schoolyard with playground equipment for the smaller children.

In the Nappanee settlement, schools also are small with a current average enrollment of thirty-three pupils. Most schools have two classrooms. The oldest of their eighteen schools is shown in plates 1.2 through 1.4. This school was remodeled twice in the sixties, adding a basement, a side entrance, updating the interior, and adding a small shed for horses. It was finally replaced by a new structure in 2000, and the building now has a full basement that is used for storage, has running water and a central furnace. Outhouses are located on either side of the building, and the playground contains swing sets for the younger children, a basketball hoop, and a ball diamond, which is well used, even during the summer months.

Until 2000, all eight grades were taught in a single classroom by two teachers, with no curtain or other means of dividing up the space except the use of a small table for each teacher's recitation area at opposite corners of the large room. This required extraordinary patience on the part of the two teachers, and attention and quiet on the part of the students. In 1997 when I visited this school for the third time in my career, all twenty-nine pupils and their two teachers made it work, and work well. The front vestibule contained a cloakroom on one side and an entrance, work area, and stairwell to the basement on the other. The school had large windows, which lit the classroom very well. Two new schools were built in this settlement in 1998, among them the school shown in plate 2.17.

The Adams County settlement has an average enrollment of forty-three pupils in each of its twenty-three schools. Most schools have two teachers. One of the older schools, built in 1970, has a current enrollment of sixty-five pupils in three classrooms (plate 2.18). This school has the third largest Amish school enrollment in Adams County. The school has a single-story frame and a full basement, but the building is elevated above ground as if it were a two-story struc-

2.17 Newer Amish School: in the Nappanee and Elkhart-LaGrange settlements most newer schools have apartments above the school for the teachers to live in during the school week.

2.18 Large, Older Adams County Amish School: notice the large windows that allow for natural lighting much of the year; softball is the Amish sport in Indiana.

2.19 Parke County Amish School: this new Amish settlement began during the 1990s and has the distinction of having the smallest schools in Indiana.

ture to allow more light in the lower classroom. Three new schools were built by the Adams County Amish community during 1999.

The Daviess County settlement has nine schools with an average enrollment of fifty-two pupils per school. As in the settlements other than the Allen County settlement, two classrooms prevail here. Plate 2.3 shows one of the earliest of these schools. Like those in most other settlements, these buildings are based on the model of the typical Indiana one-room school. Southern Indiana is much more rural in nature than the northern part of the state, and thus the Daviess County schools often sit alone on a large plot of land. Six of the nine schools in Daviess County were built in the decade of the 1960s. Two more were built by the Daviess County Amish in 1988 and 1990, and another in 1998. All of these schools employ two teachers.

Some of the newest Amish parochial schools in Indiana are also the smallest in terms of physical size. They are located in Parke County, in a very recent Amish settlement in Indiana. All five of these schools have been built since 1992. Plate 2.19 shows one of the schools, which enrolls an average of thirty pupils.

2.20 Amish Girls Play at Honeyville Elementary: this LaGrange County public school is the only one in Indiana that serves virtually 100% Amish children. At the time of my visit in 1997, only one of the 120 pupils was non-Amish. Local Amish parents help with screening and registering preschoolers, and hold several volleyball/potluck get-togethers during the year and a barbeque fundraiser every summer.

A significant anomaly in any discussion of schools that serve Amish children is one public elementary school in LaGrange County. At the time these data were collected, Honeyville Elementary had an enrollment of 120 children, all but one of them Amish (plate 2.20). The school is surrounded by Amish farms and is located at some distance from any of the small towns where the other public

2.21 Remodeled Older School in Elkhart-LaGrange Settlement: new larger windows, a new full basement, and low-care vinyl siding really bring new life to an old school.

elementary schools are located. To my knowledge, this is the *only* public school of its kind in Indiana; although many public schools do enroll Amish pupils, these children are not the primary enrollees.

Fully 62 percent of the Indiana Amish parochial schools in the five largest settlements (68 of 109) have been built since 1970; 46 percent of them (50 of 109) since 1985.[5] Thus, the need for remodeling is not yet strong. Added to this is the tendency in all settlements but Allen County to build a second school when the population gets to between fifty and sixty pupils rather than to add on to the existing school. This assures that the schools remain small, country schools. Some of the schools built prior to 1970 have been remodeled, among them the oldest school in LaGrange County (plate 1.1). Another school in the Elkhart-LaGrange settlement (built in 1967) underwent extensive renovation in the summer of 1999. This school, shown in plate 2.21, received new vinyl siding, new windows, a new side entrance, and a new basement.

The local Amish community maintains the schools. When I arrived at school on several occasions, a school board member was at work putting up new coat hooks on the boys' side of the cloakroom or fixing a door that didn't close tightly. Just before the start of school there is usually a clean-up, fix-up workday at the school attended by many members of the local community. The school is thoroughly scrubbed down, desks are repaired or replaced, windows are washed thoroughly, and a community of excellent carpenters inspects the building generally.

There is no administrative overlay in an Amish school; there are only teachers and pupils. And custodial work is done every day by the pupils and their teachers. This reflects and strengthens Amish understandings of community, of cleanliness, and of personal and corporate responsibility. Most teachers find some colorful and even witty manner of assigning clean-up duties (a chart entitled "Don't Duck Your Duties" with ducklings holding each student's name ready to be placed under the duty of the week: clean erasers, clean board, dust, sweep, pick up trash, straighten desk rows, shake entry rug, pump water).

The physical setting of the Amish parochial school keeps the children in their community with its values and its experiences. The school building is the only building erected by each church district, and thus its centrality to their belief and practice is undeniable. Here they send a sacred trust, their children, for eight formative years. And since Amish children are not baptized into church membership until several years *after* they complete school, keeping them in the community surrounded by its values during these years prior to that significant decision is very important to the Amish.[6]

Chapter Three
The Pupils

Manda's Rule is, as the first and second graders explained to me, if your pencil is shorter than your little finger, throw it away. They came up to my seat beside their teacher's desk during noon recess on the first day of my observation in their classroom. They were a group of five or six. Of course they wanted to see what I had written in my observation log, and to know if they had been good. I showed them my log, and since they had trouble reading my writing, I read to them what I had written so far. Then one little girl walked up to me and said in a very quiet voice, "Manda has a rule;" and she recited it for me. All of the children nodded their heads. We measured my pencil stub against my little finger. I explained to them that my mother had had a saying, "Waste not: want not," that I had probably learned too well—my pencil stub was only about half the length of my little finger. After I had put the stub in the wastebasket under their watchful eyes, one of them offered me her own pencil. I treasure that pencil, just as I treasure all of the other presents those children gave me that spring: a hand-decorated chain of paper loops; drawings of teapots, of horses, and of farms; a beautiful paper cross; and an exquisitely small box complete with a lid made of folded paper and decorated with horses. The generosity of children is such a compelling virtue.

We will begin our study of Indiana Amish parochial school pupils by considering the major visible difference between them and public school pupils: their appearance. Amish children wear

3.1 German Farm Woman (1960s): although the fabric differs among the Indiana Amish, you will note that the cut of clothing is the same: a Halstuch covering the upper torso, a long apron that reaches nearly to the bottom of the even longer skirt, and a head covering (Amish women often wear a scarf when inside the house and occasionally when gardening).

3.2 Sleeveless Smock: younger school-age girls wear this smock for modesty.

3.3 Upper-Grade Girl: older girls wear a dress that is even longer and has a standup collar that pins or hooks at the top.

clothing that closely mirrors that of their parents and their grand-parents, a traditional style of clothing still worn by country people in Germany into the twentieth century (plate 3.1). It is a community style that is modest as it de-emphasizes the individual.

Girls wear plain, nonprinted fabrics in colors that are like those that their mothers wear, including, black, dark brown, dark blue, gray, royal blue, and lighter shades of these colors, plus teal, violet, yellow, and wheat.[1] Fabrics range from cotton to a very beautiful shantung. The dresses usually fasten with hooks and eyes or with straight pins, usually for the upper-grade girls. There are three dress styles depending on a girl's age. The youngest girls, through third grade, wear straight dresses without pleats covered by nearly full-length sleeveless smocks that button at the back top (plate 3.2). They wear knee-length socks and black tennis shoes. In school they wear a white Kapp, which covers their ears and has long white ties that most leave hanging to the sides. In the cloakroom, they hang their

3.4 School-Age Boy: this style of shirt is more typical of the Elkhart-LaGrange settlement or Adams County settlement.

black waist-length cold-weather jackets and their bonnets. Girls in the middle grades wear below-the-knee-length, pleated dresses with aprons instead of smocks. These older girls often wear knee-length hose rather than socks. Some wear tennis shoes; others prefer black tie shoes. Girls in the upper two grades wear ankle-length dresses with bodice tops and stand-up collars, broad waistbands, and fully pleated skirts with aprons of the same fabric (plate 3.3).

Boys all wear broad-fall pants (plate 3.4) and suspenders; some boys wear clip-on white or black, nylon stretch suspenders, but most wear suspenders with leather loops that hook to buttons sewn into the waistbands of their pants, either on the outside or the inside. Shirts are usually long-sleeved with broad cuffs and are always of a single color—shades of blue, gray, brown, and occasionally green or yellow. White is worn only for Sunday preaching. I remember arriving at school a bit late one day in a white shirt, dark-blue pants, and suspenders. The upper-grade boys were still playing basketball in front of the school, and as I walked past with a friendly wave, one of the boys said, "Looks like Steve's going to church today." I'm sure I blushed, and I will certainly remember to wear a white shirt only on preaching Sunday. Boys' shirts have broad, open collars that lie flat on either side of their necks. In most settlements of Indiana, the shirt has small hooks and eyes for closure, although in the Nappanee settlement boys often wear store-bought shirts with buttons. Some mothers, and older sisters, sew the boys' shirts with a decorative yoke in the back similar to what one sees on western apparel. Boys wear black athletic shoes or black work shoes often purchased at discount stores located near their settlement. In the cooler months, boys wear short black jackets and black felt hats like their fathers; in the hot months, straw hats are typical. When they enter the school, the boys hang their hats on their side of the cloakroom and put their lunch containers on the shelf.

This uniform mode of clothing has several important symbolic functions for these school children. First, it emphasizes to them that they are always in community when they are in school. This style of dress is part of the church Ordnung, and although they are not yet members of the church, they are surrounded by this important church teaching every day. Second, it automatically takes care of all questions of modesty. There are no bare legs here, no bare midriffs, no tight-fitting clothing to lead the mind astray. These modesty issues can be seen immediately when Amish families go to town on warm summer days (plate 3.5). In the Amish school, one sees no immodest clothing. Third, there is no opportunity for aggrandizement of the self through one's choice of clothing. Where everyone wears the uniform, differences become matters of personality and facial features, not style-consciousness or wealth. Where no patterned fabrics are allowed, there is no room for ostentation, or worse, for lewdness. The dress shows that these pupils represent the community and its values. They all look like one another; and they are all working at the same thing—training the mind as they seek their God-given talents.

3.5 Elkhart-LaGrange Amish Family in Public Setting:
during the summer, the modesty differences between
Amish clothing and that of moderns is striking.

The mode of transportation that Amish children use for getting to
school varies widely in Indiana, and it is directly tied to the practices, the Ordnung, of their community. In all settlements, there are
pupils who walk to school regularly and a few who use horse-and-
buggy transportation (plate 3.6). Some children ride to school in
open carts, which will carry three comfortably, pulled by ponies,
particularly in the Daviess County settlement (plate 3.7). Some children arrive at school in a buggy driven by one of their older siblings,
although this is not common—in one school in the Elkhart-La-
Grange settlement the youngest driver was reported by the teacher
to be a fourth grader.[2] In other settlements, whose Ordnungen allow
bicycles, like those in LaGrange County and Nappanee, pupils will

3.6 Walking Home from School in Daviess County: typical of Amish parochial schools in Indiana, some children walk and others ride to school by buggy (cart, school bus, bicycle, or rollerblades— whatever the local Ordnung and school board allow).

3.7 Daviess County Pony Cart: in this Amish settlement, children can hitch up their favorite pony, put on its best harness, hitch up the open cart, and have an adventure before and after school.

3.8 Bikes at an Elkhart-LaGrange Amish School: where the Ordnung allows, a bike is a great way to get to school.

ride their bikes to school (plate 3.8). Yet others who live on paved roads, in the Allen County settlement for example, enjoy the exhilaration of getting to school using rollerblades during the warmer months of fall and spring. Most Allen and Adams County Amish pupils, however, ride school busses supplied by their local public school before the scheduled pickup of public school pupils (plate 3.9 and plate 3.10).

All Amish parochial school pupils carry their lunch. This eliminates the expense of maintaining a kitchen and a staff of cooks; when someone wants to treat the whole school to lunch, they cater it themselves and set it up on Ping-Pong tables in the basement. Some children carry their lunch in brightly colored insulated containers; some use old-fashioned lunch boxes; still others use lunch pails made from five-gallon ice-cream containers. Schools that have heating stoves in each classroom allow the pupils to heat their foil-wrapped lunches on the stove just before a wintry noon. And what a delicious aroma fills the room on those occasions, confirming the adage that having to wait makes one appreciate something more.

3.9, 3.10 Allen County School Bus:
the local public school system
makes its busses and drivers
available to transport Amish
children to their schools before
the public school begins each day.

Amish school pupils also bring snacks, most of which are too sweet and too full of fats. To be fair, most of them seem to run it off during recess; the incidence of childhood obesity in Amish schools that I have visited over the years is very low. One good way to use up that snack is to play Eskimo Tag on a winter day. Five are declared "it;" all the rest, including teachers, run around in the snow eluding them. If you are tagged, you go to the pre-established base area, where you stand hoping for release. That can only happen if someone who has not yet been tagged, comes to you, holds your hand while counting to twenty-three (impossible!), and then yells "Eskimo" to set you free.

Few Amish parochial school pupils take schoolwork home. There, they will have chores to do before dinner; like most farm families of earlier years, the Amish custom is "early to bed and early to rise." Teachers encourage responsible use of study time during the school day, and those who consistently have trouble completing their assignments during school are told to stay in and work during recess until they learn to budget their time more wisely. This is not to say that no work is ever sent home; often assignments for working outside of school involve memorizing something or writing an essay or a poem.

Amish children in schools where I have observed are often encouraged to read in their free time. And all Amish parochial schools that I have visited have a library, usually in each room, which the pupils are allowed to use if they have finished their other work, or, in the case of the middle and upper grades, if they have an encyclopedia assignment. For such work, many schools have several sets of encyclopedias in each room, including recent editions of *World Book* and *Encyclopedia Britannica* (plate 3.11). These are usually purchased by the school when they are several years old and at a substantial discount. Room libraries also contain a few books for pleasure reading, particularly for the youngest children who need practice with their reading skills. Older children usually prefer to bring their own longer reading materials to school—and this is where the opinions of teachers come into the question. What should they be allowed to read in their free time?

3.11 Bookcase in an Upper-Grade Classroom: encyclopedias, atlases, and various hymn books (for morning devotions) fill out the shelves in an Allen County upper-grade classroom.

Amish book dealers always carry a selection of books that are acceptable to even the most traditional Amish opinions. Found in many Amish school libraries are the Little House on the Prairie series by Laura Ingalls Wilder, the Miriam's Journal series and other books by Carrie Bender, and The Boxcar Children series by Gertrude Chandler Warner. These are wholesome reading for young people accepted throughout the Amish community. Carrie Bender's books are all fictional depictions of real Amish situations. Bender is her pen name, and she is a practicing member of an Old Order group in Pennsylvania. *Shagbark Hickory*, *Pineapple Quilt*, and other books by respected Amish authors like Joseph Stoll are also favorites among many Amish teachers. These books, and many Amish textbooks and teacher resources, are published by Pathway Publishers, one of the most respected Amish publishers of school materials with major facilities in Aylmer, Ontario, and in LaGrange, Indiana. No teacher questions these materials for pleasure reading; some even read them aloud to the children after noon recess.

The problem books come from two readily available sources: the public library branches in their communities and the open shelves at checkout lanes in supermarkets and shopping centers located on the edges of Amish settlements. The paperback books available in libraries or checkout lanes include books that stress romantic love, which appeal to the girls, and westerns or wilderness adventure stories, which appeal to the boys. Some children bring these books to school and place them in their school desks, out of sight, until they have finished all their assignments.

A few Amish teachers find these materials to be relatively inoffensive. After all, westerns often include excellent fictionalized descriptions of geography and even history. Many Amish boys who turned into practicing, baptized Amish fathers "cut their teeth" as teenagers on westerns. But westerns also usually have as a story line people killing people, and for a pacifist church, this is not considered appropriate for young minds. Moreover, these same westerns often contain bad language and swearing, which Amish parents find offensive, unnecessary, even an abomination. Accordingly, some teachers who find a boy reading a western will ask him to "put it away," an Amish euphemism for "get it out of sight and out of mind, and don't do it again." Some teachers also prevent girls from reading stories such as the Sweet Valley High series, which includes such titles as *Teacher Crush* and *Secret Admirer*. Such stories' romantic notions about love do not have as their basis the lifelong commitment to partner, family, and church expected of Amish adults. Moreover, some of these paperbacks openly describe physical features and physical attraction in a way that is not in keeping with Amish notions of modesty.

Amish children accept admonitions to "put away" such reading materials without argument, for that is the Amish way. Such immediate acquiescence to an adult admonition is one of the reasons that Amish schools need no administrators. The teacher is the final authority, and the child knows it.

The pupils whose work I have observed in Indiana Amish schools also showed several other personal characteristics that, although generalized, are typical enough that they could be said to predominate as the common characteristics.[3] First, these children are exceptionally soft-spoken inside the school building; though, on the playground they are as loud and even boisterous as all healthy young children can be. During class, teachers often must bend over to hear the whispered questions of their pupils. And when the children, even eighth graders, come up to their teacher's desk to ask questions about their assignments, they lean down right next to the teacher's face or even whisper the question in the teacher's ear.

Second, Amish children have a keen sense of hearing, developed so acutely perhaps because this is still an oral society, where one's words are spoken and listened to much more often than they are written or read. Teachers rarely say something more than once, and most speak at a conversational level when they address each grade level with a new lesson. Moreover, when teachers read aloud answers, to arithmetic problems during grading for example, they read very quickly. It was typical for twenty arithmetic problems to be passed forward, graded, passed back, checked, and entered into the teacher's grade book in five minutes in the upper grades, and with very few calls for repeating answers.

3.12 Middle-Grade Essays: teachers put up their pupils' essays on a classroom wall for the children and visitors to enjoy.

Third, these children have a strong work ethic that causes them to diligently do their assignment even when the teacher is working with another group. This is true with one major exception: If the teacher begins telling an anecdote, all eyes come up. The children focus their attention on the teacher until the anecdote is finished, but then they go quietly back to work without being told to do so.

Fourth, Amish pupils are definitely interested in their performance. I have seen children cluster around their teacher's posting of everyone's class ranking and grade point average at the end of the six-week grading period, and I have also seen the quietly disappointed looks on the faces of those who had to report, out loud, a grade that everyone knew was below average. Other children have drawn my attention to their teacher's spelling chart which features colorful stars beside each child's name after they attain a goal, or to the essays that their teacher has displayed prominently on the wall of the classroom (plate 3.12).

Finally, these children respond well to simple statements of correction. Not once during my visits to Amish schools did I see a child challenge an adult in even the slightest way. They listen to reprimand and correction—always given privately and succinctly—and they "mend their ways," as the Amish say. This may well stem from the fact that the entire church community works this way on those who need correction. They speak simply, plainly, and privately to those whose ways are not in keeping with Amish practice as expressed in their community. If the person modifies his or her behavior, the matter is forgotten. If not, the consequences will involve the whole faith community.

I can remember one fifth- and sixth-grade class that came in from recess early, sat down immediately, and put their heads down on their desks. They wouldn't even talk to me or come up to where I was sitting, rewriting my notes. When their teacher came in, she told them she hoped they had thought about what they had done and were repentant. That was it. She didn't lecture or scold; she relied on their sense of wanting to truly repent to carry the day, and it did. I never did learn what had caused the reprimand; she was more respectful of their need for private repentance than she was for sharing her tribulations with a fellow teacher.

During first and second grade, pupils in an Amish parochial school have to learn to curb their natural exuberance by learning not to talk out without permission and to hold their hand straight up without shaking it until the teacher gets to them. Some children have more trouble with this than do others. Jacob Adam and JoAnn were two bright, inquisitive, irrepressible second graders, who had not yet learned that talking out enthusiastically was breaking the Amish school code of silence (with no fidgeting) until spoken to.

The first reprimand I heard their teacher, Manda, utter was a hushed German, "*Schtill!*" The next time a name was used: "Jacob Adam, *Schtill!*" (To have one's name called out as a reprimand is very embarrassing.) That seemed to do the trick for that day, but I saw the same scenario acted out on several occasions, and his teacher moved from German hushes, to English commands, to loud English commands.

Jacob Adam also had another habit that annoyed his teacher, one that she knew would not be tolerated once he had moved upstairs to the third grade: his enthusiasm caused him to halfway stand up at his desk when he raised his hand. And he was not alone. JoAnn had the same pop-up, hand-waving, look-at-me-wanting-to-get-some-attention habit. Manda started with a sharp "JoAnn, sit down," but that only worked two or three times. So she had to do something else. Manda knew how to turn her back and ignore children who hadn't learned what a meek spirit means. She didn't preach or use Bible verses; she didn't yell (well, usually she didn't yell); she just turned her back to the JoAnns and Jacob Adams of second grade and made them wait an eternity—until they had forgotten what they wanted attention for, and had gone back to work. *Then* she got around to them.

Another typical problem for the first several grades is learning to be in charge of one's own belongings: "Larry, put your shoes on; you'll get your socks all dirty." Larry had left his shoes on the playground when he was rollerblading at noon recess. Now he's sitting in the classroom in his white socks, looking bewildered, because he can't follow her instructions. His teacher calls him up to her desk; he whispers his problem in her ear and pads with a red face back to his seat. She calls his brother up to her desk, whispers to him what to do, and he goes out to the playground to find his brother's shoes. The embarrassment of having to come to the front and say what he had done was enough reprimand for Larry, and Manda went on with her work as if nothing had happened.

Though hard work and discipline are fundamental to Amish practice, one final anecdote relates how cheery an interruption of hard work can make us, even teachers. The seventh- and eighth-grade girls had been dismissed at a one-room school to go to the basement to practice their roles for the upcoming school closing program. The rest of the pupils were diligently at work with their two teachers. Suddenly, from the basement, came a loudly chanted line from their program: *"Kinder, Kinder, was geht on?"* (Amish German for "Children, children, what's going on?") Both teachers giggled loudly, and soon we were all having a hearty laugh. Then everyone quickly went back to work, without a word from either smiling teacher.

Chapter Four
The Teachers

The Amish still treat teaching like a calling; that is to say, one does not train to become a certified, credentialed teacher, and then go looking for a teaching job. Instead, a member of the school board usually comes to one's home and asks if one would consider taking up the calling of teaching, at such and such school, for the next term (school year). And this visit is made only after much discussion among the school board and church officials about the Christian character and suitability of the person, including their ability to maintain discipline and to handle the subject matter.

At the beginning of their service, many candidates will be only a few years older than their oldest pupils, and they know that discipline questions are exacerbated by one's youth in a society where age means heightened respect and respect automatically helps with discipline. Moreover, these candidates usually have only an eighth-grade education, and thus, they may feel overwhelmed at the prospect of teaching subjects that they only recently learned themselves. These two issues are prominent decision factors for the school board members and for those they are calling to teach, particularly if that young person is under twenty years old.

The candidate is given some time to consider the request, and then the board returns to receive her or his answer. If the answer is yes, the beginning teacher will need to spend part of the busy spring and summer period learning how to teach and preparing the materials that are used in the grades for which she or he will be responsible. This responsibility is taken very seriously in the Amish community, and thus the candidate will feel the weight of the task heavily. Indeed, the *Regulations and Guidelines for Amish Parochial Schools of Indiana* suggests that a beginning teacher arrange to have the summer before that first year of teaching free for learning and planning.[1] The first resource for learning will be one's own former teachers and teachers who are members of one's *Gemein*, the dialect word for church community. Many other resources are also available to Amish teachers, including several works especially written for beginning teachers. (These materials and other teacher training opportunities will be discussed in chapter eight.)

The kind of persons chosen to be teachers in the Old Order Amish parochial schools is often quite different from those who teach in public schools. The Amish community would say that the primary criterion be that potential teachers be persons of high Christian character. The "test" for this attribute is their church membership and the regard in which they are held within the Amish community. The word of mouth reputation that one gains in such a "folk society," as Robert Redfield asserted over fifty years ago, is of extraordinary importance.[2] Other criteria are of secondary importance. Therefore, even though some non-Amish persons do teach successfully in their schools, it is rare.[3]

Modesty in one's demeanor, in one's attitudes, and in one's dress are considered whether the teacher is of Amish faith and practice or not. Every aspect of every day's work is completed *in der Gemein*, and this religious community emphasizes and expects from all members and from their children that they practice *Demut*, that traditional and all-encompassing attitude of humility that causes Amish people to cover their bodies, to incline their eyes rather than stare assertively, to walk slowly and deliberately, to be wary of excessive talking, to think long before they speak, to defer to authority, and to practice what they are exhorted to do in the book of the prophet Micah, who calls upon the people of Israel to "walk humbly with thy God."[4] In demeanor and attitude this means that one will not be self-asserting, or as the Amish say, "forward," or too "full of oneself." To jump in with one's own ideas, for example, is not appropriate if one's demeanor in so doing is pushy. And in dress this means that one will cover the body at all times, keeping shirts buttoned and dresses long and not tightly fitted, wearing colors and (usually nonpatterned) fabrics that are not striking or eye-catching, but rather *bescheiden*, modest and unassuming. The children and their Amish teachers all wear the traditional Amish clothing, described and illustrated in chapter three. This clothing of course makes the question of modesty in dress moot for anyone except a teacher who is non-Amish.

Another quality that is absolutely critical in a new teacher is the ability to keep order in the classroom, the feeling for discipline. Since Amish schools have no administrators, all discipline problems must be handled by the classroom teacher herself/himself, immediately and surely. And this is not an easy task, even for those who understand discipline from the Amish perspective. Numerous articles in *Blackboard Bulletin* discuss how to handle questions of discipline. Anecdote after anecdote describes the often horrific consequences of letting discipline slide if you are a teacher.

Yet another quality, that only becomes important after a teacher steps into the classroom for the first time, is personal energy. This is different from the work ethic, which obviously must be strong to be a teacher in an Amish school, or any other school for that matter. A very strong level of personal energy is required in Amish schoolteachers because they teach a minimum of two grades, sometimes all eight, and all subjects for each grade level, and they teach these grade levels in at least three subject areas every day. I have done it, and I can attest to the need for constant finely tuned attention to everything.

These aspects of personality will affect employability of a teacher candidate and success in the Amish classroom after a teacher is employed. But personality alone is never enough if one wishes to become a teacher. It certainly helps to have been reared Amish, and particularly to have attended the Amish parochial schools. However, I know some teachers in the Amish parochial schools who have attended their own Amish parochial schools (some with Amish teachers, others with non-Amish teachers), others who attended public schools, and still others who are not Amish, but Anabaptist like my grandfather, and they are all equally successful.[5] Having been raised Amish, or in the least Anabaptist, a teacher knows intuitively what the expectations are, what the problems are, what the curriculum is like, and even what a typical day's work will be. Most Indiana Amish teachers I know have a formal education through the eighth grade; some have expressed a desire for additional formal education, and all with whom I have interacted attend informative teachers' meetings on a regular basis and/or read articles on pedagogy in *Blackboard Bulletin*.

Regardless of the teacher's personal background, one must be willing and able to study hard and learn right along with one's pupils; to grade all the work that students churn out under their direction; to play actively with the children on the playground at recess; to counsel pupils and their parents; to interact with the school board; *and* to find some other way to supplement one's income, at least during the summer months.

One of the continuing problems for the Indiana Amish schools is attracting and retaining teachers for their schools. The pay for teaching is not enough in itself to support even a single person without additional employment. Although I do not have information on current practice, information from the Elkhart-LaGrange settlement nearly ten years ago, a time when beginning public schoolteachers would have earned about $18,000, indicates that young Amish teachers earned about $5,000 per year—a salary that was supplemented by minimal housing arrangements during the school week and by a stock of canned foods supplied by the families of the schoolchildren.[6] Therefore, in the Amish community, the potential teacher usually must have some additional means of support or be living with a large extended family that provides this basic support to them. Most men can earn far more in typical Amish work environments for men (skilled carpentry, masonry, factory work, and other skilled trades typical in the Indiana Amish communities) than they can earn as schoolteachers, even when they supplement that income with home businesses, micro-industries, or skilled trade employment during the summer months. This economic factor is very real, and there is little expectation that the amount of "teacher money" that comes in to teachers every month from the families of their pupils could rise enough in the near term to make it possible for one to support a family with this work.[7]

Living arrangements for Amish schoolteachers vary with their age, marital status, and with the settlement in which they teach. Those who are older and married will, of course, live with their family, usually in the district in which they teach. Thus, their transportation to school is by horse and buggy or on foot when the weather permits.[8] Unmarried teachers in some settlements are sometimes housed in apartments above the school. This is particularly true of newly constructed schools in the Elkhart-LaGrange settlement (plate 2.17). Here the distance is so great from one side of the settlement to the other, approximately twenty miles, that daily buggy travel is virtually impossible because of time considerations. These efficiency apartments for teachers allow the occupants to cook, wash, and do other everyday activities as well as to sleep, and they offer a measure of privacy and of comradeship with other teachers not usually available if one finds lodging with an Amish family. Often two or three young women room together during the week in their apartment above the school and return to their parents' homes for the weekend (using hired transportation). Other unmarried teachers who cannot drive or walk from their homes, live for the school term in a nearby Amish home where they can have a room of their own and meals at little or no cost.

In the Allen County, Adams County, and Nappanee settlements, most Amish teachers are able to drive a buggy to school, since they live no more than several miles from the school. The greatest problem with buggy travel in all three of these settlements is that a major highway, a heavily traveled two-lane road, bisects each of these Amish communities. Many drivers drive at or above the speed limit of fifty-five miles per hour, and there is only a blinking caution light at one major intersection of an artery used by the Amish. I know teachers who must cross such busy highways every day on their way to school. I have seen driving horses get unruly having to wait to cross; I have seen one horse bolt at an inappropriate moment. Several times in winter, when the roads were very treacherous, I have seen large trucks bear down unmercifully on Amish buggies, frightening both horses and their drivers. I often thought on my way to school that I would arrive exhausted and shaking if I had to cross such roads early on a winter morning.

Amish schoolteachers in Indiana range in age from about eighteen to over sixty years (the youngest and oldest teachers whose work I observed). In the Allen County settlement, for example, the average age of the fifteen schoolteachers during the 1997–98 school year was thirty-four. Of this group, ten were women, average age twenty-six, and five were men, average age thirty. The youngest teacher was eighteen, and the oldest teacher was fifty-two.[9] Among the five male teachers, four were in their thirties and one was nineteen. Among the women, four were either eighteen or nineteen years old, four were in their twenties, one was in her forties, and one was in her fifties. Each of the four older men is considered to be the head teacher in his school, and he teaches the upper-grade pupils. It is interesting to note that more Amish men are now teaching as their primary occupation, although they supplement their income from teaching with other income-producing work. The fact that there are no women in the Allen County settlement teaching in their thirties can be explained by the fact that Amish women often marry in their early to mid-twenties and will be bearing and rearing their own children during these years. It is very common in this and in other settlements for there to be a predominant majority of young women teachers in their early twenties who teach for three or four years and then marry and quit teaching.

The ratio of women to men teachers has changed over the period of my lifetime. Early in the Amish parochial school movement, there were comparatively few male teachers; although the number of men teaching today is still low, their numbers are growing. We will compare the numbers of men and women teachers in the five largest settlements that account for approximately 90 percent of

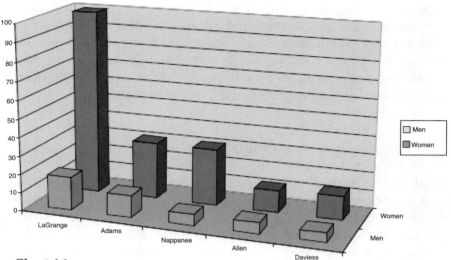

Chart 4.1

Amish parochial school enrollment in Indiana. During the 1999–2000 school year these five settlements employed 234 of the total 271 teachers in Indiana.[10] Of these, 80 percent were women (187) and 20 percent (47) were men.

Chart 4.1 gives a graphic representation of the numbers of men and women teachers in each of the largest five settlements during the 1999–2000 school year. The Elkhart-LaGrange settlement employed eighteen male (15 percent) and one hundred female (85 percent) teachers; the Nappanee settlement employed six men (16 percent) and thirty-one women (84 percent). In the other three major settlements the percentage of male to female teachers was significantly higher. In the Adams County settlement, they employed twelve men (28 percent) and thirty-one female (72 percent) teachers; in the Daviess settlement, five male (28 percent) and 13 female teachers (72 percent); and in Allen County, six male (33 percent) and twelve female (67 percent) teachers.

What is it like to be a beginning teacher in an Amish parochial school? Among the nineteen teachers that I observed in 1997 were three beginning teachers. Two were in their first year of full-time teaching; the other was in her third year. By the time I reached their classrooms, all had completed the first half of the school year and had settled into a routine with their pupils. All three of them were teaching very competently; one was an extraordinarily gifted teacher of phonics. Two of them were young Amish women; one was a young Amish man. The two young women taught first- and second-grade pupils in basement rooms; the young man taught fifth and sixth graders in an annex.

Manda, one of the first- and second-grade teachers, has a delightful way of making her basement classroom inviting to young children who are leaving Mom and Dad behind, using English all day instead of Deitsch, their home dialect of German,[11] and learning all the important skills that many children find difficult to master. In chapter three, where we profiled students, you read several anecdotes about her sense of the psychology and heritage of her pupils.

The other young beginning teacher who works with first and second graders was then in her third year of teaching, and already she had developed a presentation on phonics for the first graders that was masterful. On one day when I was in her classroom, she was presenting the long vowel sounds followed by what I had always called the "*e* marker." She said, "This is called a magic *e*." Now what child doesn't like magic! And to harness that magical power for reading is irresistible! Using a large flip chart that she had made of the various orthographic possibilities, she first had the children look carefully at the letters and model her pronunciation.[12] Then they wrote several words using the "magic *e*" on their own papers. Finally, she displayed a large chart of words that used this construction and asked the children to pronounce them with her. These colorful and large charts that she had painstakingly prepared before class made it easy to see that there are indeed some rules in English pronunciation that are worth learning.

I also had an opportunity to watch this same young woman interact with her children on the playground at recess. She didn't stand back and watch. She was an active part of every game; but she also saw to it that no one was left out and that no cliques could get started. Several times she left the game for a moment to have a chat with several who wanted to stand around together and point and laugh. They were soon running with the rest. And when the children got tired of one game, she immediately had another to suggest: "Did anyone ever play Pom Pom Pull Away?" They were out of breath, rosy cheeked, and happy when the bell rang, and they settled down immediately to their reading lesson after recess. That day after school there were first and second graders literally surrounding her desk as they waited for their busses to arrive. That they adored their teacher was clear; that they had learned from her went almost unnoticed to them.

This profile of the teachers in the Indiana Amish parochial schools will close with a bit of wisdom that I learned from an established fifth- and sixth-grade teacher. Children at this age are beginning to experience physical changes that also affect their mood. They also must have mastered the math tables and become proficient readers by this time, and that adds additional stress in their lives. This teacher knew intuitively that the best reminders that we are in charge of our own responses to life's pressures are anonymous and unspoken. On her front bulletin board she had placed the following thought: "Life is a mirror. If you frown into it, it frowns right back at you. If you smile at it, it smiles back too."[13]

Chapter Five

Leaving Home
and Learning the Basics
in Grades One and Two

The *Regulations and Guidelines for Amish Parochial Schools of Indiana* stipulates that Indiana Amish schools will offer all grades two semesters of the following subjects: reading, writing, spelling, and arithmetic. However, each local school board may or may not also choose to offer penmanship, phonics, health or science, and/or German. Each school board interprets the *Regulations and Guidelines* for itself and sets the particulars of the curriculum. Arithmetic, reading, and writing are the focuses of learning in grades one and two.

In large Amish schools, where enrollments often exceed one hundred, grades one and two usually are taught together by one teacher in her own room. If there is a basement room at the school, it often is used for these two grades. Smaller Amish schools usually house grades one to four in one classroom that contains about thirty children and the upper four grades in another classroom with a teacher of their own. The smallest Amish parochial schools in Indiana teach all eight grades together in a single classroom of about thirty children. In some of these small schools, one teacher is responsible for all grades; in others, this responsibility is split between two persons, each working with four grade levels on her or his side of the one-room school.[1] Regardless of the setting, I have found that the first grade receives extra attention from their teacher and extra help from upper-grade pupils, or from mothers whose husbands sit on the school board, as the need warrants.

This chapter, as well as chapters six and seven, will feature one Amish parochial school, which I will call Baugo Amish School. Where other Indiana Amish schools differ in their approach or materials, I will comment as appropriate.

At Baugo School, grades one and two are taught together in a basement room that has more than half of the wall structure above ground so that the basement rooms can have large windows to let in light and air as necessary. There are fifteen second graders and thirteen first graders in this room. Their teacher certainly has her hands full meeting the needs of twenty-eight tender little souls, all of whom are struggling to learn what it means to work a full day without constant and immediate attention from their mother or father (or their teacher). By the time they reach the afternoon class period, the first graders especially are very tired and their attention spans are just about exhausted. To get them ready for that last work period, she reads aloud to the entire class after noon recess, while they may rest their heads on their desks if they wish. She reads a full chapter, or even two, if they seem interested, from *Farmer Boy* by Laura Ingalls Wilder, a book in the Little House on the Prairie series that would be beyond their own limited reading ability at this point. They relax; they rest or even daydream; and they improve their passive vocabulary in English, their second language, and learn how a good reader sounds. Teachers of middle-grade pupils also read aloud to their students after noon recess, and some of them allow the children to quietly work on special projects like knitting or crocheting while they listen.

Manda, as she is called by her students, is a young Amish woman in her first term of teaching and responsible for grades one and two at Baugo School. As we saw in chapter three, she is making a strong beginning as a teacher. In addition to her interest in teaching, she is also a very talented seamstress, has many wonderful ideas about how to build a sense of community among her group of little learners, and incorporates an artistic sense of decoration in the classroom

5.1 Amish Boy-Bear Quilt: hung on the entrance wall of a first- and second-grade room; opposite the boys was a wall of girl bears. Each bear was made by the boy and his mother to represent him in the classroom.

setting. One of her decorating touches, a quilt of boy bears and girl bears who welcome you to their classroom, is shown in plate 5.1. Manda has cheered up their room with other touches of home. In one window she has a ceramic watering pot with plants, a little basket with fragrances, and other objects that remind her and the children of good times (plate 5.2). Near the entrance of the room she has put up stencils of flowerpots that the children have colored and signed in their best printing. Other teachers bring in scented candles and burn them so that they will release a pleasant scent to accompany the hard work. Yet others keep a jar of mints or even Jolly Ranchers on their desks as an open invitation to enjoyment—in moderation, of course.[2]

5.2 **Window Decorations:** to remind her pupils of home, this beginning teacher decorates her classroom like her own home.

For Valentine's Day, Manda sent two upper-grade girls (one of them her sister) with me to an Amish store to pick up several yards of fancy white lace so that her children could decorate the edges of their Valentines—always addressed to Jesus—like those beautiful designs made by the pupils of her colleague Elizabeth in the middle-grade room (see plate 6.1). This was a good example of making the most of what you have at hand: Steve was there; he had a Jeep; she knew two older girls who would love to take a break from school, even if it meant they had to ride in a Jeep; they knew which neighboring Amish farm had a dry goods shop in the rear; and in twenty minutes her class was adding beautiful lace ribbon to their paper valentines.

5.3 Amanda's Soup: another touch of home
on a cold winter's day.

At the front of the room behind Manda's desk, is a library of
reading books; a shelf system where her pupils know they are to
place their workbooks for grading when they have finished them; a
large chalkboard with an English alphabet in script and in block
print; a math chart and a calendar above the pencil sharpener. Behind this area is their cloakroom. At the back of the room is a metal
picnic table with a Formica top and benches where she takes the
children for reading. Beside the table is the large heating stove for
the colder months, which Manda also uses occasionally for cooking
a pot of delicious soup for her entire class (plate 5.3)—another
touch of home.

The school day in Manda's classroom begins with the Lord's Prayer led in German by the teacher herself. This is often followed by some pupil being asked to say the date, and by announcements: "Starting today you boys are supposed to take your rollerblades off upstairs—before you come down here." (The noise of rollerblades on stair steps was unbelievable.) On another day early in February, Manda asked, "Does everybody have your shoes on and tied?" After a quick check under the desks, she continued: "Now everybody set their cracker box beside their desk, and I'll come around later and tape them on for you." The cracker box, tastefully decorated in a personalized style, would serve as each pupil's own wastebasket, so that the floor doesn't look like a tornado has blown through by mid-morning. Announcement time is followed by a story or by singing. The songs usually are religious in nature, and often are memorized since these young pupils are just learning to read. Occasionally, Manda's pupils will join Elizabeth, the third-, fourth-, and fifth-grade teacher, and her pupils to sing together.

Primary-grade teachers read aloud to their children several times a day, in the early morning and after noon recess. The choice of reading material is the teacher's own, but most will begin the morning with Bible stories rewritten for small children or with stories that have a moral-ethical lesson. These stories are always in English and may have been used in the teacher's own home when she or he was a child. Manda reads from *Uncle Arthur's Bedtime Storybook*. She begins with "Amy's Gift," the story of a girl who gives her own doll away to another girl whose doll had been crushed under a truck. She interrupts herself to ask, "What's a parcel?" After the children answer softly, "Package," she finishes the story. Afterwards she asks, "Did anybody's mom read this story to them?" The answer is immediate—and German, "*Ja, ja.*" Then she reads a second story entitled "How Donald Missed His Dinner," at which the children laugh heartily. They keep laughing because Donald arrives home after school with a message to Mom that he forgot where he left his shoes, his cap, and his books. (It is comforting to know that someone else slips like you do, and that this time you can laugh about it without getting in worse trouble.)

After story time, Manda tells everyone, "First graders, keep quiet a couple minutes until I get done over here [meaning with the second graders]. Get out arithmetic. What page are we ready for?" A first grader softly answers, "Twenty-nine." Manda looks at the page carefully and sees that it is a review, so she says, "Okay, you do that page while I work with the second." And she turns to the second-grade arithmetic lesson, completing it before she gets back to her first graders. Arithmetic and learning to read and write English are the hardest subjects for the first grade, and they receive a very strong emphasis in terms of time. Manda begins every school day with arithmetic.

Arithmetic

The first-grade arithmetic text is entitled *Learning Numbers With Spunky the Donkey* and was developed in 1995 by Schoolaid, an Old Order Mennonite publishing house started by a group of retired Amish and Old Order Mennonite teachers from the Pennsylvania parochial schools. It is a paperbound, two-volume set. The second volume, *Learning More Numbers with Spunky*, is intended for the second half of the first school year. This series has been widely adopted by Amish schools in Indiana for first-grade instruction.[3] There is a teacher's guide for the series that gives detailed information on how to present each page, so a beginning teacher has tremendous support from authors who are seasoned teachers in similar schools.

The text has a delightful format. It is an arithmetic book that is also a coloring book. Page one of the first volume introduces Spunky the donkey pulling a wagon of hay—a large picture that the children are to color, underneath is a series of items they are to circle if they appear more than once (only the hay bales do). The first volume teaches addition and subtraction through the fives; numbers through three hundred; concepts such as greater and less than; and making change with coins. Late in the volume, after the children have learned to read, the authors introduce story problems. The second volume extends addition and subtraction through the tens, and the numbers through the 990s. It also introduces fractional parts; ones, tens, and hundreds columns; addition and subtraction problems; clock time; odd and even numbers; and measurements. And it extends the concept of story problems. All of the images and concepts come directly from an Amish child's life, and many of the story problems are meant to make the child chuckle: "On the bench were four hats. Three hats were bumped off. How many hats are left?"[4] *Learning Numbers with Spunky* is a simple Amish solution to teaching math: The printing cost is low because the text is in black and white; the children provide the color as part of their work.

One young woman relates that she had struggled with the concept of telling clock time in first grade. When she was in the second grade, she again watched her teacher introduce this concept to the first graders. She said that she listened intently, and that the extra repetition made all the difference. The fact that she remembered this moment so poignantly nearly twenty years later demonstrates the real advantage of having multiple classes in the same room.[5]

The other major learning of first grade involves what for these children is a second language. Learning to read and write English means leaving home in a sense that many other American first graders would not understand. These first graders have spoken a home dialect of German (although many have heard and even spoken English as well), a way of communicating that they must put away when they go to school; some teachers require that the children use only English even during recess for the first half of the school year.[6] Because they must acquire a second language and develop fundamental literacy skills at the same time, two subjects from the English language arts group, reading, phonics, or writing, are taught every day. We will look first at the reading curriculum.

English PreReading (Reading Readiness)

Since Old Order Amish children enter school speaking Deitsch as a home language and some of them have only limited exposure to English before they reach school age, English reading is a very significant task for both teacher and pupil. All teaching is conducted in

English, but several teachers have remarked that a deep understanding of German is very helpful in order to understand the types
of mistakes pupils make, to be compassionate with their struggles
and to make contrastive studies of pronunciation problems between
German and English, i.e. *w* and *v*, *d* and *t*, *v* and *f*.[7] One Amish first -
grade teacher had written the word *gay* on the board during a phonics lesson on long *a* in English; she asked the children what the word
gay means, and one boy immediately held up his hand and glossed
it as "Go!" She laughed and shook her head and said, "No, Marvin,
that's what our German word *Geh* means in English."

First graders generally begin with a seatwork book and phonics
workbook that provide a basic English vocabulary of items common to Amish life and phonetic tools for pronouncing and understanding the words as lexical items distinct from similar words. One
popular seatwork book, written by an experienced Amish teacher
and published by Pathway Publishers, is aptly entitled *Helping
Yourself: A Seatwork Book for First Grade*. Seatwork involves teaching
entering first graders several important aspects of classroom work:
(1) to sit still, hence the subtitle; (2) to work without immediate
direction and without constant attention; (3) to follow oral instructions delivered to a group; (4) to color within the lines; (5) to paste
without making too much mess; and (6) to learn to coordinate work
with one's eyes and one's hands—a necessary practice for learning
to read. But the text also teaches subliminally. For example, when
the initial sound of the letter *u* is practiced, the correct answer is *ugly*
and the corresponding picture is the face of an angry, pouting child.
The community value system would say that anger and pouting are
self-serving prideful behaviors that make you ugly. This is called
Hochmut—one of the worst sins of Amish belief and practice.

English Phonics

Toward the end of the first grading period teachers begin phonics
instruction using a series of two workbooks from Pathway Publishers, *Learning Through Sounds Book One* and *Learning Through Sounds
Book Two*. *Book One* begins with a series of pictures of words that

have the same initial sound. The children are asked to repeat after the teacher: *cat—corn, butterfly—buggy,* etc., as the English alphabet is introduced. In a note to the teacher, the authors make clear that they have chosen pictures with which "the average Amish child is familiar."[8] By the end of *Book One,* the children build whole words using letters. *Book Two* introduces consonant blends, long vowels, consonant/vowel digraphs, and diphthongs. By the middle of the book, the children recognize the International Phonetic Alphabet signs for long and short vowels. By the end of *Book Two,* these children, whose first language is German, are reading their own directions, reading full anecdotes, and completing exercises that test their understanding of difficult English spelling conventions. One of the last anecdotes describes a first grader named Sam on an adventure that ends—as many do in real life—with productive work:

> Sam made a dash for the shed. What do you think he saw there. The chicks had hatched! For three weeks the mother hen had sat on her white eggs. She ate the wheat and drank the water Sam brought to her each day. When Sam found that nest, he shouted for joy. He went to check on them almost every day. Now he had a bunch of little chicks.[9]

These authors understand a first grader's need for excitement, and they also know the value of bringing an occasional smile to the face of a hardworking student. One sentence that the children are to correct reads: "We had brain flakes for breakfast."[10]

The introductory phonics books also come with a very well-crafted teacher's manual that teachers are encouraged to read thoroughly before the school year begins. It contains detailed instructions for introducing and completing each lesson and detailed pedagogic discussions of significant issues in teaching phonics, such as the need for drilling, teaching sounds before letter names, and an excellent anecdotal discussion of phonics vs. whole word instructional pedagogy. The anonymous authors of these volumes want children trained in this method to be able to read effectively during and after their school years: "Children who say, 'I like phonics' will in a few months also say, 'I like reading.' This, after all, is our goal— to lay a solid foundation for further learning. We all know, a good reader is usually a good student and needs much less teacher help the rest of his school years."[11] And the teacher's manual for the next two stages of the prereading phase are equally full of sound pedagogy and deep understanding of the teaching and learning process:

> The attitude with which children tackle their lessons is often a reflection of their teacher's attitude. Therefore the importance of showing enthusiasm can not be overstressed. From the very first day of school, children should be guided to look forward to the time when they can read. You might say, "Won't that be nice when you can read stories all by yourself?" Learning should be an interesting, challenging experience that lasts even beyond the time the pupil attends school.[12]

English Reading

Following work with prereading and introductory phonics, first and second graders move on to a series of English readers published by Pathway Publishers. Their reading series includes four books for first grade and two for second grade. Many teachers have each pupil stand beside the desk and read aloud a passage, correcting pronunciation occasionally and helping with more difficult words that students seem unable to sound out. Others follow Manda's practice of moving all of the first graders to a picnic table at the back of her room. This provides a more family-like setting and helps quiet the nerves since everyone can read while seated. Each pupil recites, even the slowest (unless the pupil requires special education help), and then the teacher asks all the first graders (or second graders, if they are reciting) a group of content questions based on the day's assignment.

The first reading book, a preprimer, is entitled *First Steps*. In this book the children read about their "Reading Book Family,"[13] most of whom they met earlier in their seatwork and phonics workbooks. This reader and accompanying workbook about Amish family life involves both the children and their teacher in read-aloud exercises. Each of the first four reading selections has a several-page anecdote about the family that the teacher is to read aloud to the pupils on the day before *they* are asked to read. The drawings that the children see are black and white and comport directly with an Amish child's everyday experiences. They show a horse tied up to the side of a buggy shed with a buggy sitting behind it ready to be hitched up. The situations, too, are ones that Amish children would know and look forward to. One anecdote, read to them by their teacher, features a father and his young son having an enjoyable experience—going to a horse auction to purchase a driving horse. The teacher's story ends at exactly the point where the children's story will begin the following morning—with the introduction of Bess, the brown horse who likes children, to the two youngest children in the family when Dad and Peter get home.

The next several selections are about a little red wagon that the children receive and then lose until they learn that they must also include their baby sister in their play. Following this lesson are several readings about things that the children observe: a cardinal, a turtle, clouds, cows, flowers from the garden that they pick for the table, and cookies that Mother has baked. A subsequent story deals with the children wanting to ride on the hay wagon with Dad, and the fact that the two younger children must follow Mother's admonition that they play with the baby rather than getting to ride. Their having to tend the baby instead of having fun and their reconciling themselves to this fact become a leitmotif in the book to which virtually every Amish first grader can relate. That is their duty at home when Mother needs to do something else. The story continues with the children eating popcorn on their little table outdoors, and when they leave to play, the cat eats their popcorn and knocks over the table. (Although I can't show you a photograph, I'm certain you can imagine the wide eyes and giggles that this anecdote causes.) Reading becomes a vicarious playground for the mind's eye. The children learn to know Bess's new colt and give it a good name. The younger children work fast for Mother shelling peas from the garden, and receive a reward from Dad from the store for their fast work, a lollipop. Indeed, fast work is the goal in several stories.

Another set of readings deals with new kittens in the barn. We find that a rainstorm keeps the children in the house at Mother's firm instruction, but Rachel's desire to run to the barn overcomes her and she disobeys her mother. After seeing that Mother doesn't have a happy look on her face at the window and hearing Rachel's confession, Dad sends Rachel back to the house. But Rachel becomes a happy girl when she realizes confession was right. Heavy handed, you may say. Well, consider the context. Amish children, in the words of an old hymn from the 1880s, learn to "trust and obey— for there's no other way, to be happy in Jesus." And for those of us who don't know it, barns are dangerous places, particularly in stormy weather, for large animals can be very excitable. Moreover, many of us know from watching adults in our religious practice, at least in Catholic and Protestant traditions, that confession is good for the soul. This child has been disobedient and caused her mother to become angry and worried—and what child hasn't. Moreover, cute, little kittens are a temptation for nearly everyone I know. These Amish children are getting a good dose of child psychology mixed in with a bit of "horse sense." This lesson extends well beyond childhood for Amish children because it will be their obedience to the Ordnung that will distinguish them someday as adult members of the Amish church. In the course of teaching a variety of moral and ethical lessons (sharing, obedience, thrift, helping out) and introducing age-related chores, *First Steps* also introduces over one hundred new words.

The primer and reader used during the second semester of first grade is a series of two books from Pathway Publishers, again designed specifically for Amish pupils, entitled *Days Go By* and *More Days Go By*.[14] The school owns each of these hardbound texts; the pupils purchase a softbound workbook for each reader. *Days Go By*, the primer, introduces 117 new words using stories that have content similar to those discussed above. *More Days Go By* will finish the work of the first grade by adding an additional 159 words in a like number of pages. By this time, many stories are six pages in length. One story from the middle of the text is particularly instructive for us because it reveals Anabaptist understandings of self. It is entitled "Laughing at Levi" and tells the story of a typical first grader who is so interested in being the first one done with his coloring that he makes a big mistake:

The children in Grade One went to work. Levi worked fast. He wanted to be done first.

Levi colored the barn red. He colored the sky blue and white. Then he colored the tree green.

Levi did not think about what he was doing. He was thinking about getting done first. Levi did not color the cow black and white. He colored it green.[15]

His seatmate looks at Levi's cow and laughs; soon the entire class is laughing, even the teacher. Levi's face gets red, but he doesn't cry; instead, he starts right over with a new page, and gets it right. His seatmate thinks to himself at the end: "The next time I do something funny, I will not cry. I will laugh at myself."[16] Haste makes waste, as we all know; and learning to laugh at oneself is a good exercise in humility. I have seen Amish teachers give instructions like this to a class: "Let's get out our new math books!" Nothing happens. The teacher looks up, and only then notices the consternation on the children's faces. She chuckles, and says: "Oh my! [another chuckle] I forgot to get them from the storeroom!" Her chuckling at herself is infectious, and we all join in.

There are three readers used in the second grade: *Busy Times*, *More Busy Times*, and *Climbing Higher*. By the time second graders have reached the end of their last reader, they are expected to manage a thirteen-page, densely printed, two-part story called "Cows Are Cows" that describes the extraordinary everyday adventures in a boy named Marvin's life. For those of us who, as children, had to learn to feed greedy calves without crying over the spilled milk; to get an escaped, giant cow back into the barnyard where it doesn't want to go; or get the "Stupid pigs!"[17] (those are Marvin's words, not mine) back into their pen, this last story is both a delight and a warning of future summer vacation possibilities.

English Writing

Reading is one major part of learning English in grades one and two. The second major task is to learn how to write this new language. The English writing series used in most Indiana Amish schools is entitled *Climbing to Good English*. The children use a workbook, and the teacher has a manual that includes the student workbook pages, answer sheets, and most importantly, a detailed and excellent teaching guide for each lesson. These materials were developed by anonymous authors and published by Schoolaid.

The text for first grade suggests that pupils begin working with *Climbing to Good English* starting in the fourth or fifth week of school. The language skills and elements taught in this first-grade English workbook include: sentence parts (verbs, nouns, and phrases), sentence punctuation (periods and question marks), rhyming words, synonyms, antonyms, homonyms, compound words, contractions, plurals, suffixes, syllables, alphabetical order, and writing original sentences and paragraphs. By the end of the school term, first graders are completing multi-sentence descriptive compositions. In the second grade, they will write letters, book reports, and will finish stories like the following, started for them by authors who know how to get any country child's blood flowing:

> One morning when the children came to school they had a surprise. A very bad smell greeted them. "Skunk!" they shouted, holding their noses. It didn't take the boys long to discover a newly-dug hole under the porch. Did Mr. Skunk think he could live there now. The boys all agreed to one thing. They must get rid of him. But how?[18]

English Spelling

The spelling text used in Indiana Amish schools was first released in 1956 by Ginn and Company.[19] The publisher gave the Old Order Amish permission to reprint and to revise their text for use in the Amish parochial schools. This work was done by the School Supply Room in Gordonville, Pennsylvania, which also distributes the series to Amish parochial schools throughout the United States. Each text in the series is entitled *Learning to Spell*. For all but the first grade, there is a hardbound textbook that is owned by the school and a softbound workbook that each pupil purchases. Weekly lessons introduce five new words in the context of linking words and pictures at the top of a workbook page, and offer a reading selection, a short cloze exercise, and an alphabetization exercise at the bottom of each page. This work is then extended in the second grade. Notes to the teachers encourage them to give the German meaning for each word and to use German-English drills to help their students learn the meanings of the English words.

English Penmanship

The Gordonville Print Shop has also reprinted a penmanship series used in Amish parochial schools from grade one through grade eight. The first-grade penmanship booklet is thirty-two pages long and teaches block printing of both uppercase and lowercase letters. The context of the illustrations would suggest that the text derives from rural America in the 1930s.[20]

The Amish parochial schools of today have as their focus the old reading (plus phonics), writing (plus spelling) and arithmetic—the core subjects taught in Indiana from the turn of the last century in one-room country schools. The Old Order Amish parochial schools in Indiana choose the old way, but with many new texts.

Chapter Six

Molding Proper Scholars in Grades Three, Four, and Five

In addition to requiring two semesters of reading, writing, spelling, and arithmetic each year, the *Regulations and Guidelines* dictate that each school must offer one semester of history and geography, a subject area that most schools begin in grade four. Learning to read German typically begins in grade four as well, after the children have firmly established their language skills in English. Health or science also enters the curriculum in the middle grades, often in grade five.

As we continue our look at Baugo Amish School, the teacher of grades three, four, and five, whom I will call Elizabeth, has framed her schedule with a pair of hands labeled "Clean hands" and "A gentle touch" and the words "Surely we owe our books that much!" Elizabeth has an eagle eye for things that need to be done better; the tenacity of a badger that doesn't allow things to slip past when that would be the easy way out; and the generous heart of a mother quail for guiding and protecting her flock of thirty-three. It was Elizabeth who helped me light my lamp on the first day I substituted; it was Elizabeth who reprimanded my boys for running through the school during recess (when I should have done so, but was too involved with subject matter questions to think of this

6.1 Valentine's Day: Elizabeth's classroom is decorated with the thoughts of her fourth, fifth, and sixth graders on the meaning of Valentine's Day.

other teaching); it was Elizabeth who worried that the books some pupils were getting at the local branch of the public library were not appropriate reading for young Christian minds and who brought in books like *Shagbark Hickory* for them to read in their free time; it was Elizabeth who had her pupils decorate their room for Valentine's Day with cards of their own making, each one dedicated to God (plate 6.1); and it was Elizabeth who made lunch for her entire class of thirty-three and served each one personally as a Valentine's Day gift—and as a lesson in making change, of course. Elizabeth, like many Amish women, is an excellent cook and an equally talented seamstress. She is often asked to sew wedding dresses and baptismal dresses for young women in her community. She is also a gifted, experienced teacher who has children of her own, two of whom are still in school.

The daily schedule for the third-, fourth-, and fifth-grade room hangs on the east wall as you enter the classroom. It reads:

Monday	Math	Spelling	English
Tuesday	Math	German	English
Wednesday	Math	Reading	Workbook (Health)
Thursday	Math	English	Phonics
Friday	History	Final Spelling	Penmanship

The school day in Elizabeth's classroom is almost always patterned like this. The children enter and sit down quietly within three minutes after she has rung her handheld bell out the doorway. (She has been encouraging them to be even more prompt after the bell.) She says a loud and cheerful "Good morning!" and the class responds in turn. If their response is not very enthusiastic, she says, "Let's start over—Good MORNING!" Then everyone stands as one of her pupils recites the Lord's Prayer in German. One of the younger children goes to the calendar in front, marks off the day, and announces to all, "Monday, February tenth." Elizabeth uses the devotional period to read aloud to her pupils from an inspirational text, and occasionally to have them sing from the blue songbook, *Country Gospel Hymnbook II*. Following devotions, the work of the day begins, patterned the same unless there is a two-hour school delay on account of bad weather: subject one from about 9:00 to 10:15; recess for fifteen minutes; subject two from about 10:30 to 12:00; at 12:00 the children are dismissed briefly to get their lunches, they return to their seats and the Lord's Prayer is recited by one of the pupils, all eat silently for about ten minutes, the Lord's Prayer is recited again, and they are dismissed for noon recess that lasts forty-five minutes; at 1:00 they begin the work on their third subject, which lasts until the busses arrive at 2:20. Most days begin with arithmetic, so we will begin our discussion there.

Arithmetic

Elizabeth is very concerned that her pupils at Baugo School have mastered the basic foundational skills that are so critical to their

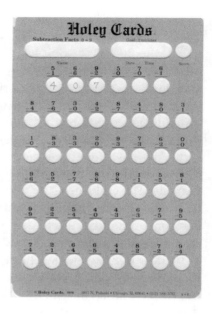

6.2 Holey Cards: a great tool to help students memorize their math facts and become proficient adders and multipliers.

success in the upper grades and later in life. On several occasions, Elizabeth said to me that her third graders did not yet know their math tables for adding and subtracting and multiplying, which are the basis for the division tables. To set these math facts in their minds she uses several different methods.

One method that is very effective with her third graders involves flash cards and team contests. Rows three and four each line up; the first member of each line is shown the flash card (7 x 6) and the first person to get the answer right scores a point for that team. The teacher says, "Yes, seven times six is forty-two." These two contestants then go to the back of the line to wait for a second turn. The children play this game with great intensity, and since their teacher has them play nearly every week through the entire set of cards, they have heard the entire multiplication table many times over; the same is true for addition and subtraction.[1] She varies the contest by having the boys go up against the girls.

Another aid for checking and practicing these facts is the series called "Holey Cards," a single card for each of the four skills with problems on each side and a hole for writing the answer on your own sheet of paper (plate 6.2).[2] Each set of one hundred problems is timed; the goal is to complete them correctly within two minutes. Elizabeth has the entire classroom take this skills test. The children love contests, and such events allow those whose skills need to be sharpened to have a bit of anonymity as they do so. If she sees that someone is slow in reciting the tables, she models the speed they should strive for, and then says, "Noah, you should be able to go about that fast. Just because I'm a teacher doesn't mean you can't say them that fast. You should be able to. Rows three and four, let's see how well you can say them." This takes the immediate pressure off of Noah, who joins the other fourth graders in their recitation of the tables. She lets them finish and then adds, "This is a practice; we'll come back and do this again and again."

Elizabeth is also the teacher who decided to sharpen her pupils' money-counting, addition, and subtraction skills by having them "buy" their lunch on Valentine's Day—the lunch that she prepared for them herself (bologna sandwich, macaroni and cheese, chips, cupcakes, lemonade and punch). She told each pupil what the lunch would cost depending on what they wanted on their sandwich ("Barbara, your lunch will cost $1.38."); and the money collected would be sent back home. In effect, Elizabeth supplied all the food at her own expense and gave the children not only a lesson in counting change, but also a good time as well.

Most of the schools that I visited during the 1997–98 term were still using the Strayer-Upton series *Practical Arithmetics Book One* and *Practical Arithmetics Book Two*. This series was developed by two professors at Columbia University, one a mathematician and the other a specialist in math education. They developed this series for the American public schools in 1928. It was reprinted in 1989 for use in the Amish parochial schools by the Old Order Book Society. *Book One* of the text covers both third-grade and fourth-grade materials; *Book Two* is for grades five and six. The original preface from 1934 states that the series "follows the recommendations of the National Committee on Mathematical Requirements and the yearbooks of the National Council of Teachers of Mathematics."[3] The pedagogy is excellent; the math is excellent, as you might expect. The only real drawback to the Strayer-Upton series is that the problems all are based on the economic realities of the 1930s when gasoline, for example, cost nineteen cents a gallon!

Baugo School has now joined others in switching to the Beka Books series for the middle and upper grades, entitled simply *Arithmetic Three* for third grade, *Arithmetic Four* for fourth grade, and so on through eighth grade. All of these books reflect the realities of Christian education in the 1990s. They are paperback; they are full of brightly colored illustrations (too gaudy and therefore worldly for some Indiana Amish schools); and the text is rich with scriptural and inspirational citations. For example, *Arithmetic Four* quotes first Thessalonians as part of the first review: "And that ye study to be quiet, and to do your own business, and to work with your own hands, as we commanded you."[4] Every teacher that I know has fervent wishes on this point! The twenty-two fourth-grade arithmetical topics presented in the Beka Books series begin with review and then proceed into the new material: place values through millions; checking addition with carrying; checking subtraction with borrowing; multiplication tables through twelve; division tables through twelve; work with story problems; averaging and estimating; converting between metric and English measurements; Roman numerals through one thousand; solving problems containing fractions; finding the greatest common factor; finding the least common multiple; divisibility rules; decimals; money problems (making change); reading the thermometer; solving equations with an unknown number; graph reading; scale drawings of maps; geometric shapes and figures; finding perimeters using formulas; and finding areas of squares and rectangles.

Elizabeth teaches math as the first subject, four days a week, for the sake of repetition and at a time when her pupils are at their best. Let's sit in on her work with the fourth graders on their math for one morning. Her first step is to grade their assignments, which she does by reading aloud the correct answer as they grade the paper of the person seated in front of them. She reminds them at the beginning, "If it's not labeled right: it's wrong." One problem reads: "How much change do you get from a five dollar bill if you buy a spool of thread for $.18, buttons for $.33, and linen for $2.78?"[5] As she reads the answers, she walks up and down the two fourth-grade rows checking their grading. When she sees that most have the problem wrong, she has two pupils come to the board to do the problem under her watchful eyes and ears. She insists that they state aloud what process they must use to get the right answer. After she is satisfied with their board work, she continues grading the assignment with the fourth grade. She uses her EZ-Grader to determine what the percentages will be, and then tells her class, "Two wrong will be 94 percent; three wrong will be 91 percent; four wrong is 88 percent." They quickly figure out what their scores will be and report them to her when she calls their names. Several raise their hands to ask what fourteen wrong or nineteen wrong will be. She looks perplexed as she tells them, "Fifty-six percent and 41 percent." In fact, the fourth-grade scores on these subtraction story problems don't suit her at all (88, 82, 56, 41, 100, 88, 88), so she says, "I was thinking we'd go on to multiplication, but with missing this many, we need to do the next page, too." Her thoroughness pays off for the upper-grade teacher, who loves math; the pupils that he receives from her are all very well grounded in math facts; in working story problems; in writing out all the stages of their answers, including long division; and in labeling their answers.

English Reading

The third, fourth, and fifth grades all use readers from Pathway Publishers, entitled: *New Friends* and *More New Friends* (third grade); *Building Our Lives* (fourth grade); and *Living Together* (fifth grade). Each comprises a hardbound reader, all copies of which are owned by the school, and a softbound workbook that each pupil purchases. The nearly 500-page fourth-grade text of *Building Our Lives* will serve as our example. It contains both poetry and short readings with very few illustrations, all of them black and white. The materials are divided into six units with titles like "Learning by Living," "Learning from Animals," and "Growing Stronger." The main characters are young people the age of the reader. The stories regularly alternate between boys and girls as main characters. All are shown in a typically Amish family setting, and the story content focuses on issues of growing up Amish: learning to enjoy work; learning to be unselfish; learning to follow the small inside voice that tells right from wrong; learning to be satisfied with what is given; and learning to reach out to others. All issues are presented in a context that stresses obedience to parents and teachers and enjoyment of time spent at school.

Several stories are illustrative of the types of lessons to be learned through reading. "Jingling Quarters," which has eleven pages with three small illustrations, tells of two boys, one just rich enough to have learned to make fun of those who are poor. This is an important reflection as this is a known problem in Amish schools, where the only cliques seem to involve children from backgrounds of money and/or influence and those from poor families.[6] As the two boys go for a walk, they find two old shoes on a bridge left there by a poor boy who was hunting frogs to sell with his friends. The rich boy wants to teach the poor boy a lesson by throwing his shoes in the water. However, his companion is a quick thinker, and he suggests that the rich boy put a quarter in each shoe, just to see what will happen. When the younger poor children come back they are astonished and talk about how they will now be able to buy a coloring book and crayons for their little sister who must stay in bed with rheumatic fever. Amish children know very well that catastrophic medical costs can make a rich family poor. They have attended auctions and other benefits for community members who needed financial help to pay for cancer treatment and other expensive medical procedures.

And "Worse Off Than Wilma," which has fifteen pages with three illustrations, features a young girl who was hit by a car on her way home from school. Now she must lie at home with her leg in traction as her siblings and friends go "merrily" to school. Her aunt sends her a box of sunshine cards so that she can write to cheer up other people who are much worse off than she. The first idea is her own: sending a picture scrapbook, which she will make, to a learning-disabled child in her community. And that primes the pump. Soon she is even receiving suggestions from parents of the other children at school—and thank you notes and visits pour in from those to whom she has written. The time flies by; and she forgets to be bored as she heals.

The eighty-eight-page workbook for this fourth-grade reader contains a series of exercises and questions for each reading. The exercises on the story "What Love Will Do" are illustrative of the others. Pupils must match definitions to a list of ten words (sausage, tumbled, tumblers, mocking, discussion, crude, harvest, rejoice, sickles, sheaves). Then they must use a form of these words to complete sentences such as: "_____ crops is a very busy time for everyone."[7] This is followed by an exercise in which pupils change an underlined word in a sentence to its antonym. Finally, pupils complete an entire page of content questions, listing both the page and the paragraph where the question is answered before writing their own answer "with a good sentence."[8] Other exercises work with prefixes and suffixes, with finding the root word, and with defining the main idea in a paragraph.

During class, Elizabeth has her pupils stand beside their desks and read aloud from the text. Occasionally, she will ask content questions or make brief comments herself about the story line. She expects good diction and reading with inflection rather than in a monotone. She provides an excellent example herself, since she often reads materials aloud to her entire class, particularly passages from their various history and geography texts that she finds especially interesting. She loves to read, and her pupils learn to as well. However, the fourth graders find reading particularly challenging, so she sometimes takes them to the basement spare room (used for Ping-Pong at recess) to read, as she says, "in peace and quiet." This sensitivity to their awkwardness and tender personalities, and her equally strong trust of her other two classes to do their work quietly without causing trouble while she is away, is a sign of an experienced, able teacher in control of both discipline and learning.

English Writing

Elizabeth uses the third-, fourth-, and fifth-grade versions of *Climbing to Good English,* the Schoolaid text used in Manda's class, for her pupils. The format is the same: a paperbound textbook/workbook that the students purchase. Beginning with grades five and six, teachers use a spiral-bound volume of the annotated teacher's edition that combines two grades in one instructor's volume (i.e. five with six, and seven with eight).

The authors make clear that the fourth-grade curriculum in English must mark a turning point in the pupils' learning curve, so we will use it for our examples. We must remember that for most of these pupils English is a second language, not the primary language. Thus, the first three years must be devoted to an accelerated acquisition of English in an English language immersion context. In their introduction to the teacher, also printed for the pupil to read, the authors set the agenda for this new phase of learning English:

> English in grade four has, to a large extent, moved out of the phonics phase and more deeply into the writing phase of language. This brings with it the many rules included in the mechanics of a language, often called grammar. When we speak of grammar, we speak of rules for capitalization, punctuation, proper sentences, parts of speech, and correct use of words and terms. The study of all of these things helps us to better understand what we read and hear, but is especially necessary to be able to express ourselves clearly. Our goal in English, then, is to better understand and communicate with one another, both in spoken and written language, in the business world as well as in our social life.[9]

The text is set up for one-room schools that teach English three days a week, but they supply a set of practice sheets that allow teachers—as they recommend—to teach English every day. After a brief review of what was taught in grade three, *Climbing to Good English Four* practices: kinds of sentences; the grammar of English verbs, including irregular forms and agreement of subject and verb, and usage questions; nouns, pronouns, and adjectives; writing para-

graphs, including order, proofreading, and citation; finding information in dictionaries and encyclopedias; more advanced verb
studies, including active and passive, prefixes and suffixes, and adverbs; letter writing; writing poems and prose paragraphs; writing
outlines and reports; and improving one's compositions. The text
ends with a review of capitalization, punctuation, verbs, nouns,
pronouns, adjectives, adverbs, and other grammar questions.

Many lessons contain sample sentences that reflect Anabaptist
understandings of positive behavior: "Did you do a kind deed
today" (Lesson 10); "Silver and gold tarnish and bring no happiness" (Lesson 15); "Obedience is the greatest gift you can give your
parents" (Lesson 53). Other lessons provide review of troublesome
grammar items like learning to distinguish between *to* and *too*, *its*
and *it's*, and among *there*, *their*, and *they're*.

By Lesson 43, the fourth graders begin writing longer compositions such as news stories, stimulated in this case by a newspaper
article about a mule that ran loose through New Holland, Pennsylvania. The authors' keen sense of what makes life interesting to a
fourth grader and their ability to apply that to an English lesson is,
as one of my Amish friends would say, "awesome." I can recall one
day when I arrived at school to hear about a beautiful driving horse
that had been found dead on the road that morning; and I can remember another day on the way to school when three horses, two
huge Percherons and one naughty driving horse in the lead, gal-
loped down the road ahead of me "testing the breeze" with their
tails up as high as they could go.[10] By Lesson 96, the fourth graders
will be asked to list three major events in their life, and then to write
a long paragraph composition based on their notes.[11]

Lesson 70 is taught early in the second half of the school term. It
involves the pupils in letter writing, a composition with a different
purpose. The lesson includes two sample letters written to Justin,
who had an operation on his back and lies in a hospital. One letter
grumbles about pain and about how tiring it must be for Justin to
have to lie in bed; the other tells about what has been happening in
the neighborhood, and closes by saying that the author is keeping a
log of all assignments for Justin and that the baseball team can

hardly wait until he returns. The authors ask pupils to decide which letter Justin would appreciate more. We should note again that the authors are teaching more than just the rudiments of punctuation in English; they are also asking pupils to make a quality of life decision based upon the needs of someone other than themselves. This moral/ethical premise for all learning pervades virtually every lesson in the text and reinforces the Anabaptist heritage of these pupils, whether they attend Old Order Amish or Old Order Mennonite schools.

Elizabeth grades thirty-three worksheets and compositions from three grade levels in the evening and on weekends. Her remarks to the fifth grade on a Tuesday are like her approach to the third and fourth grades as well: "Fifth. Just be sure your English books are turned in. I'm not assigning any more lessons today, so be sure they're turned in. Hand in your reports also for English." By the end of the day, one corner of her desk is piled high with thirteen fifth-grade English workbooks and a like number of essays that she has ready to hand back the next morning—with the exception of the essays, which she deems so good that she puts them up on the back wall of her classroom "so everyone can enjoy them" (plate 3.12).

When Elizabeth teaches the fourth-grade lesson on writing friendly letters (Lesson 70 discussed above), she surprises me by saying, "The reason you put all caps on an envelope is because they are read by computer." Being Amish doesn't mean that you ignore what is happening in the world; it means that you evaluate what is happening, accepting some things and rejecting others, deliberately. She goes on to suggest what several fourth graders might want to write about: "Amos might invite Jacob and Steven for a cookout. And Susanna might invite her friends for a birthday party." Then she begins to tell a story about herself, and all eyes look up to her: "I had to give a presentation once on first-year reading, at a teachers' meeting at School One. I did it by writing a friendly letter to former teachers. [brief pause] When you are done put your books up here on a pile." Simple, heartfelt, humble, to the point! And she ends with an indirect reference that they have work to do, which they begin, immediately.

English Spelling

Baugo School, like numerous other Indiana Amish parochial schools, uses *Learning to Spell* versions for grade three, grade four and grade five. All of the hardbound volumes are owned by the school; pupils purchase the accompanying workbook. This spelling series, originally copyrighted in 1956 by Ginn and Company, was used in the public schools of Indiana and across the nation. The series was revised and reprinted by the Old Order Amish in 1990 with permission and is now available from the School Supply Room in Gordonville, Pennsylvania.

The fourth graders, for example, will learn 510 new spelling words, 16 new words every week during the first half of the year, and 18 words per week during the second half of the year. Reading exercises use the new words in context, arranged in units, each with its own theme, e.g., "Children in Foreign Lands" and "A Trip Across the United States."

The fourth graders read aloud each lesson in the hardbound book, and then the exercises are assigned for later in the week. The teacher discusses difficult exercises before they are assigned. The new words are always pronounced, as are the review words and the other useful words. Elizabeth assigns the words in these three lists to be memorized for her "final spelling" class on Friday, when she gives them as an exam. On Friday, she tells her pupils how many words they will spell; then she says each word and uses the word in a sentence. They check the exam together as a class and then report their grades. Amish children love to spell; they are very good spellers who participate energetically in spelling bees.

On Tuesday, after noon recess, Elizabeth's entire class has a spelldown, class by class; and she gives out new pens, which she bought, to the three winners. Other teachers reward achievement with certificates, "Mighty Multiplier," or gold stars for brushing their teeth every day.[12] For the spelldown, the fifth graders stand and go to the back, boys on one side, girls on the other. Elizabeth asks them to stand in alphabetical order, which they do instantly. She begins by stating the rules, "You must pronounce the word;

then you have two tries." After six rounds, only one person has had to sit down; after ten rounds only three are sitting. So she has to go on to a lesson that they haven't studied yet, Lesson 30. The children whisper loudly, "Ooh!" and Elizabeth beams. After thirty minutes, we are down to the last two, both of whom miss the word *column*. The winner is Maureen, with the word *permission*.

Then it's time for the fourth, as she calls them. They stand up at the back of the room in alphabetical order, boys on the right and girls on the left—as they know to do. She says "Lesson 24" and begins to say a word, then stops, and says, "Oh, I was ready to give you fifth-grade words." A rather loud whispered "No" from the group of seven fourth graders follows this. Those who miss must sit down and watch. Eventually, Susanna wins her new pen by correctly spelling the word *automobile*.

History

Elizabeth loves to travel, and she uses this to great advantage when she teaches geography and history. When her fourth graders reach a unit on desert landscapes in their text, *The World and Its People: States and Regions*,[13] she says, "I want you to write down some words: *rainforest, lakes, bare earth, sunshine.* Which of these words remind you of a desert? [She waits for their answers.] Now we are going to read about a desert in the West, the Painted Desert. When my husband was young, he visited the Painted Desert. I'd love to go see it. I'll have to look at home to see if I can find the Viewmaster of the Painted Desert." Then she reads aloud, and interprets. She especially enjoys a passage where the Navajo first see some Amish and think they look like Pilgrims. She says, "Let's learn about the Navajo people. Would you like to be a Navajo child for a few days? Wouldn't it be fun—for a few days—to live like an Indian?" All thirty-three children are by now watching her avidly—not just the fourth graders—and all nod their heads enthusiastically. She continues to introduce the new fourth-grade geography lesson, with the rapt attention of the third- and fifth-grade as well.

This method of allowing interest to direct the attention of everyone from time to time works very well. The third graders are learning some facts early; and the fifth graders get a chance to review something that they learned last year as fourth graders. Elizabeth often reads aloud from the fourth-grade text or from the fifth-grade text, *Great Names in American History*, to her entire class. She has a delightful way of moving from one class to another; she says, "Well, fifth. It's your turn. Let's have history. When I was a little girl, John Schwartz used to say 'Okay, let's have high story.' That's just a joke, because of the way it's spelled, but it does make you think." Then she continues with their lesson on mountain men like John Fremont and Sam Houston.

On another day she decides to begin not with the traditional devotional period, (because they have lost two hours on several days this week due to snow delays) but rather with a modified geography reading that she uses as a platform for talking about living issues of Christian faith. She begins to read from the fourth-grade geography text, *The World and Its People,* a public school text published in 1984 and now distributed by an Indiana Amish book dealer, about farming in the (former) Soviet Union.[14] She soon interrupts herself to say, "Before I read on, we know that they have changed in the last years, and our books haven't been updated yet. Just the other night, I watched a program on the changes in Russia today at a friend's house. They are having to work hard to learn how to produce their own food. Like Mary's dad milks a lot of cows, and he gets his own check from the co-op for the milk." Then she returns to her reading, but interrupts herself again from time to time, to tell them how to pronounce difficult words, to explain things to them, or to add comments: "You all know I'm interested in herbs" or "If you drink purified water, it has all the minerals taken out." It becomes clear to them that she is reading this text aloud to them just as she would read it to herself—with interest and full of questions and comparisons with her own life. Such open, honest, personalized mentoring is typical of all her teaching.

German

Indiana Amish parochial schools vary as to when they introduce German into the curriculum. Its purpose is to help them read and understand the Luther Bible. Although a few schools start German in third grade, Baugo School begins in grade four. The two texts used by Elizabeth's fourth graders are the *Erstes Deutsches Lesebuch*, a hardbound text owned by the school, and *German Phonics*, a workbook that the pupils purchase.

Erstes Deutsches Lesebuch was first "entered according to Act of Congress, in the year 1887, by Lauer & Yost," according to the original copyright page, and is now revised and reprinted by Raber's Book Store in Baltic, Ohio.[15] The first twenty-five pages are an introductory series on the lowercase letters of the German alphabet, introducing how they are written in script and in *Fraktur*, ornate block script used in the Luther Bible. Pages twenty-five through fifty-eight practice the uppercase and lowercase letters and introduce short reading passages, with interlinear glosses in English.[16] Lesson 17 describes the arrival of the mail—by vintage steam engine. Many of the readings contain favorite German poems sung by mothers and fathers in Germany to their children even today as nursery rhymes, including the *Steckenpferd* rhyme and the rhyme of opposites. This section also contains a number of religious readings, including the text of the Christmas story from the Bible, the story of Simeon, Jesus in the temple, the Sermon on the Mount, the Ten Commandments, and several prayers.

The paperbound workbook *German Phonics* was developed by Pequea Publishers, an Old Order Amish publisher, in 1983. It was developed with the Amish schools in mind, and thus its pictures and readings reflect the Amish way of life.[17] The authors explain that they use an approach that fosters learning and memorization, an approach in which the pupils first see the word (or sound) as the teacher says it aloud; then they say it aloud themselves and write it into their workbook. At the same time that they learn German phonics, they also increase their vocabulary. At the end of the text is a glossary of over six hundred words that the children will have mastered by the end of the year. We must remember that, although

6.3 German Fraktur, German Script, and English Alphabets Adorn the Front
of a Middle-Grade Room: literacy in German, i.e., learning to read the Bible in
Luther's Fraktur, begins in fourth grade—after the English language is firmly
established—and continues through eighth grade.

they speak a dialect of German, this is the first time that they are
learning to read, or are becoming literate, in the standardized form
of ecclesiastical German developed by Martin Luther. Luther's six-
teenth century translation of the Bible was so successful that it standardized the German language.

In class the children read aloud from each text and learn to mimic
the teacher as she pronounces words and phrases for them. Elizabeth
also likes to have the children memorize texts, especially prayers and
passages of Scripture and sayings, in German that they must then say
aloud to the class, or to her at her desk if they are too embarrassed.

At the front of the middle-grade and upper-grade classrooms is
an alphabet in Fraktur, and the upper-grade classrooms—where the
school is divided into more than one room—have an additional alphabet in German script as well (plate 6.3). Many pupils like to

copy the alphabets in their own writing, and use it to write out passages of Scripture in their free time. This is particularly helpful with Fraktur; it is a script form that requires some practice before one can readily distinguish the *f*, *s*, and *t* letters in lowercase.

Elizabeth enjoys talking with her pupils in German from time to time during the German lesson. She speaks Deitsch, a dialect similar to Pennsylvania German, to them, and they speak Dietsch, a south German dialect of Amish, similar to Swiss German, back to her. From time to time, they all giggle about her word, or their word, or her way of saying this, or theirs. This difference is peculiar to the Amish living in Allen County and Adams County, Indiana, many of whom have intermarried and find that one spouse speaks Dietsch and the other, Deitsch.

English Penmanship

The Gordonville Print Shop penmanship series is also used in Elizabeth's class. Its creation in the 1930s is evident by the pictures of boys and girls assuming the correct position for writing, the pictures of scenes from American life, and the description of the pens and ink that pupils should use.

The fourth-grade booklet is entitled simply *Penmanship Four*. All eight books in this series have basically the same format, and each of them has its own theme. At the top of each page is a script written in cursive that students copy repeatedly onto a sheet of paper until they feel they are ready to enter it into their copybook. There are occasional instructions on how to form some letters and admonishments to practice good posture and to form their letters using certain movements of the pen. These comments are always in typewritten block letters to distinguish them from the text to be copied.

The thirty-two pages are meant to be completed one per week. Students receive no real instruction in penmanship after the initial strong emphasis in the lower grades, but they are expected to do the work and to turn in their books once a month for grading. Elizabeth has her pupils pile their books on her desk on the Friday before she intends to grade them.

English Phonics

At Baugo School the third and fourth grades are the last grades in which English phonics are taught. A workbook entitled *Phonics We Use: E* is used for this instruction. Lyons & Carnahan first published the Phonics We Use series in 1946 for the public schools of America, with the copyright last renewed in 1964. Since that time, the Gordonville Print Shop has reprinted the series with permission. Volume E is intended by the original publishers to be used with fourth-grade readers. The entire series ends with the sixth-grade text; some Amish schools in Indiana use this volume later, as late as the eighth grade, but Baugo School ends its phonics instruction during the middle years, in the fourth grade, with Volume E.

This approach to phonics instruction is very thorough and quite effective. I have taught a phonics approach to German pronunciation for many years, and would be delighted to have a similar text to use with my students. The teacher need only follow these directions explicitly and the pupils will have gained an exceptional sense of how phonics may be applied to the English language. All of the teachers I observed teaching phonics with this text used the teacher's edition and its suggestions to guide their work.

Health

Pupils at Baugo School begin health instruction in grade three. *Health Trails: Grade Four,* also owned by the school with an accompanying workbook that pupils purchase, provides the fourth grade instruction in health. Laidlaw Brothers originally published the text in 1957 for the American public schools. Since 1976, it has been reprinted by the Gordonville Print Shop, which also released the workbook in 1977.[18] This text, although originally used in the public schools, is old enough to date back to a time when general ideas of modesty still comported with what current Old Order Amish sensibilities would consider acceptable. That is to say, the approach taken here is general health: cleanliness, healthful living, proper nutrition, care of teeth, safety, and first aid. There is no discussion of reproduction and of birth control options.

The workbook supports the general content in the textbook and provides significant reading practice for the pupils. There are many matching exercises for word study; cloze exercises; and a number of long readings on topics such as the negative effects of drinking alcohol or smoking tobacco. The workbook also contains chapter tests that significantly lighten the burden of preparation for the teacher.

These subjects and years prepare these students for that important last opportunity for an Amish schoolteacher to help pupils develop the skills and attitudes necessary for living a full and productive life in the Amish community.

Chapter Seven
Preparing for Life after School in Grades Six, Seven, and Eight

The eighth grade is the end of formal education for most Amish children, but it marks the beginning of a lifetime of learning on the job. Thus, it is critically important that upper-grade pupils extend their learning into the working world in several key areas, particularly in the famous "Three Rs," reading, writing, and arithmetic. For this reason one teacher in the upper grades who loves arithmetic has made several changes in his math textbooks over the past three years, from the Strayer-Upton old standard used in most Amish parochial schools to a series called *Basic Mathematics* developed by Beka Books during the 1990s, and then again to a brand-new text by the same publisher that he had to special order directly. Its eighth-grade math book has as its focus practical applications of math for the working world, specifically bookkeeping and tax accounting. We will consider this topic in greater detail later in this chapter, but for now we need to realize that teachers consider seventh and eighth grade to be their last chance to help these children perfect their knowledge.

In some schools, the seventh and eighth grades meet together with one teacher; in others it is the sixth through eighth; some combine grades four through eight in one classroom; and in yet other schools all eight grades meet together in one room. At Baugo School the three upper grades are combined in one classroom: nine sixth graders, eleven seventh graders, and eleven eighth graders. The eighth graders sit together in two rows on the east side of the room, the five girls near the wall and the six boys in the row beside them. This separation of boys and girls reflects a typical separation of the sexes among the Amish in worship, and even some informal settings such as the home.

This group of thirty-one pupils is taught by an Amish man, whom I will call Andy. In his thirties, Andy has not always taught school. His talents have gradually involved him in many kinds of work. He supports his family through a successful micro-industry, capably managed by his business and life partner, Anna, and worked by the entire family. Their hard work and intelligent management allow him now to devote himself during the academic year to what he loves—teaching school. He is a truly gifted teacher, one whose pupils reciprocate his love and care for them in many ways. On his birthday, the eighth-grade boys caught him after they were dismissed to get their lunches. All six ganged up on him and squeezed him under his desk—where his feet normally would be—while the whole room sang "Happy Birthday" to him. This is acceptable behavior on a birthday, a sign of their affection for their teacher. A noon meal catered by school parents and an afternoon program completed the day.

The upper-grade curriculum is essentially uniform in all of Indiana's Amish schools. Pupils learn reading and writing in English, and arithmetic as their primary subjects. These subjects are supplemented with lessons in spelling, history, geography, health, science, and German for reading the Bible with understanding. In comparison with the subject matter covered by a teacher in the public schools, where one instructor usually covers one subject, at the most two, this is a daunting task for the teacher.

Andy's weekly schedule for the upper grades is on a colorful chart at the back of his classroom. Although the schedule might differ somewhat from one school to the next, Andy's upper-grade schedule seems to predominate currently in Indiana:

Monday	Math	English	Reading
Tuesday	Math	English	History
Wednesday	Health	German	Spelling
Thursday	Math	English	Reading
Friday	Math	English	History

In this classroom math and English are taught four periods per week; reading and history are taught two periods per week; and health, German, and spelling are each taught one period per week —all three on Wednesday, which makes a nice midweek break from the "hard" subjects. Moreover, Andy has decided that the long morning should be devoted to the two major subjects; then follows the long noon recess; and the day ends with an easier subject, because the children are more tired by this time and less able to concentrate on hard thinking. This is good psychology, and it also reflects the typical Amish pattern—and that of most farm families of my youth who regularly recited adages such as "Early to bed, early to rise, makes a man healthy, wealthy, and wise," "The early bird catches the worm," or "Make hay while the sun shines." Moreover, the easier afternoon subjects and the shorter afternoon lesson plan leave pupils feeling upbeat rather than burned out as they leave school for the day.

Every day follows the same pattern, and its regularity becomes an order to which pupils and their teachers soon adjust. Teachers will occasionally deviate from this pattern when they have special guests or when they are preparing for one of several programs at Baugo School, which the pupils give for the community (Christmas and School Closing), or when there is a two-hour school delay for fog or for snow. There are enough of these unscheduled changes to keep a school year varied. The pattern for a typical day in Andy's upper-grade classroom is:

8:50	Bell
8:55	All stand; one pupil says the Lord's Prayer in German
8:56	Devotions (for the entire classroom)
9:30	Math

The eighth grade works first, while the others complete their homework assignment; the pattern is always the same: grade the assignment; report the grades; introduce the new lesson; give the assignment; then the pupils begin their work on their assignment while Andy moves on to the next class. All of this work takes about twenty minutes; that leaves another forty minutes for the pupils to complete their math assignment. When all classes have recited, Andy sits down as the signal that students may now raise their hands and come up to ask questions.

10:40	Recess
11:10	Bell
11:15	English (following the same pattern as math)
12:05	Noon recess

All the pupils are given time to wash up, to get their lunch, and return to their seats; this is followed by a silent prayer; then the students eat their lunch very quietly and quickly; then there is another silent prayer; then they are dismissed for recess.

1:30	Bell
1:35	Reading (repeating the pattern of math and English)
2:18	Busses arrive
2:20	Dismissal

Each school will have a different typical daily pattern, and lower-grade teachers will follow an order that is more suitable for their classrooms.

Order is very important here. Order is evident on the blackboard, with eighth-grade assignments and clarifications on the left, seventh grade in the middle, and sixth grade on the right. This in turn reflects the order of their seating. And their seats have always been arranged in orderly rows by their teacher when the pupils enter every morning. The books on the teacher's desk are arranged in

7.1 **Long Ranger EZ-Grader:** a tool used by many Amish teachers to make
the grade-recording process more efficient and timely.

three orderly groups, positioned in front of each grade level. The
grading and presentation sequence followed by the teacher shows
distinct order as well. Andy first stands up and walks over to stand
in front of the class that he will work with. Then he reads aloud the
page number(s) and correct answers of yesterday's assignments.
Next he asks if there are questions about the grading. Then he walks
back to his desk, sits down, opens his grade book, takes out his
Long Ranger EZ-Grader (plate 7.1), and calls the first name of the
first eighth grader, arranged alphabetically by last name, "Jonas."

He tells the pupil what that percentage score is, "Ninety-three percent." After all grades have been entered, he stands again and moves over to stand in front of the group. Then he gives the page number for the next day's assignment, waits a moment, and begins reading aloud the instructions. Following this is the one moment when he might ad lib, namely to answer any questions that they might have about what they are to do. The end of his work in this subject with the eighth graders is marked by his returning to his desk and sitting down. While he is seated—but before he has stood up to present the seventh-grade lesson in that subject—all his pupils know that they may come to his desk, stand quietly in line, and ask him any questions. They do not need to hold up their hand; they know that this is allowed, at this time. There is a rhythm to this order of work, one to which the pupils quickly adjust. This rhythm is no different from that involved in other kinds of work that they will do: swinging a hammer; baling a field of hay; hitching up a horse and buggy. And the orderly progression of the daily work in school reflects their name, Old Order Amish, and their Ordnung, the German word *order*, to which they will agree at baptism and that determines what their practice as Amish will be. Such an expectable, reliable order of classroom work must surely also have a positive effect on issues of discipline.

These students work quietly and diligently when they have study time, and grading is completed very quickly. My impression, based upon many hours of observing upper-grade pupils and several days of teaching them, is that they are expected to treat the time in school much as one would treat time spent at work—with diligence, attention to detail, efficiency, and not too many questions. Even in a classroom where pupils are allowed to consult with one another during study time without specific permission from their teacher, such consultation is done very quietly and with little movement, certainly none that would draw the teacher's attention.[1] Such responsible behavior is expected from all pupils, and it is the teacher's duty to establish and then to require strict adherence to behavior standards at all times, and to punish those who disobey or show disrespect. These high expectations, established early in life, account for the high reputation that the Amish have as reliable, careful, self-motivating, and fast workers.

Arithmetic

The eighth-grade curriculum will be our focus in this classroom, because it is the last formal schooling that these young people will have. We begin with mathematics. Most schools still use the old Strayer-Upton series *Practical Arithmetics*, as Andy did until 1998. *Book Three* of this series covers both seventh-grade and eighth-grade materials. The preface from 1934 defines what kinds of mathematics are contained in the book, and it gives us a real sense of the history of math education:

> The applications of arithmetic as found in business and industry, as well as those encountered in personal life, are presented in such a way as to make them real and interesting to boys and girls of the upper grades. Special attention has been given to such topics as banking, modern business practice, accounts, budgets, thrift savings, investments, insurance, installment buying, purchasing a home, and taxation.[2]

The text teaches concepts of solid geometry, algebraic equations, graphing, and problem solving and includes nearly one hundred diagnostic tests.

Book Three is a hardbound text owned by the school. Each eighth grader has a copy of the text, minus the answer sheets at the end, which Andy has cut out with a razor-blade knife so that he has the only copy with an answer key. The eighth grade begins their work in the middle of the text, with a chapter on the formulas for finding areas of rectangles, triangles, trapezoids, and circles. This will be reviewed and extended one hundred pages later as they present the formulas of solid geometry. I have seen major portions of this text used in the Indiana Amish schools taught by several teachers, and I can say without equivocation that this is a challenging approach to basic applied mathematics, similar or perhaps identical to that used in the public high school that I attended in the 1950s. The story problems are quite challenging, but the eighth graders whom I observed worked diligently and quickly through the problems, which they solved longhand without calculators; Andy also requires that they use a checking procedure on their answers. For example, the exercises assigned on the solid geometry problems include this story problem:

> Last night John dreamed that he was painting the Great Pyramid of Egypt, which has 4 equal sides, each having a slant height of 593 ft. and a base of 746 ft. If its sides were entirely smooth, what would its lateral area be? If John took 1 hr. to paint 100 sq. ft. and worked 8 hr. a day, how many days would he take to paint the Great Pyramid?[3]

The percentage grades on arithmetic exercises for the eleven eighth graders, whose work I know best, were uniformly in the high nineties. Andy is a continuous student of math himself, and so it is no small wonder that he loves to challenge them with extra assignments from reproducible homeschooling materials available at most teachers' supply stores and with occasional problems that he dreams up for their edification. One problem that he had hand drawn and then copied for the eighth graders constituted a belt and pulley system that would be hooked up to a stationary engine running at 2200 rpm. Students were given a diagram of the setup; the sizes of the *twelve* pulleys; other critical measurements; and several formulas, for example, "to find speed: speed of shaft x pulley size ÷ by next pulley size." They were to solve it for the speed of the shaft at the end, given in rpms, but were to show the speed for each of the intermediate shafts as well as the sizes of the belts "to the nearest whole number in belt size because you can only buy one length"—a bit of practical reality. As is usual in all Amish parochial schools, the pupils may not use a calculator (although instructors do for calculating end of term grades). The eighth graders did very well on this applied learning problem; I on the other hand, who had attempted to do the problem with them, earned a 68 percent.

English Writing

Like the math text, the eighth-grade English text is also teamed with materials developed for the seventh grade. The softbound student text for the eighth grade is 286 pages in length. It was published in 1992 by Schoolaid, the Old Order Mennonite publishing house, and is entitled *Climbing to Good English Eight*. As I have explained elsewhere, this is part of a rigorous series of English texts that begins in grade one. The eighth-grade student workbook concludes with a forty-page handbook of English that is meant to serve as a guide for their writing long after they have entered the world of adult life and work. I have taught intermediate composition as part of a "writing across the curriculum" venture for many years at my university, and I can say that the English curriculum is superb. The work in English is strong, in part because it reflects the standards for American public schools at a time when many, if not most, citizens had "only" an eighth-grade education.

English Reading

The sixth-, seventh-, and eighth-grade English readers were published by Pathway Publishers. The eighth-grade text, entitled *Our Heritage*, is 476 pages in length and contains seventy poems and fifty short stories arranged into eight thematic units: Our Heritage, True Values, People who Served, Thinking of Others, Nature's Wonders, In Olden Days, The Way of Love, and Home on the Farm. Authors include, among others, Henry Ward Beecher, William Cullen Bryant, Lord Byron, Fanny Crosby, Emily Dickinson, Edgar Guest, Rudyard Kipling, Henry Longfellow, Alfred Lord Tennyson, Walt Whitman, John Greenleaf Whittier, and William Wordsworth; thirty-eight of the signed works were written by women. Many of these authors wrote during the period of Romanticism, when belief in a beneficent God, in the inherent goodness of man, and in the restorative power of nature held full sway. That the Amish still read and memorize works by such authors accounts in part for their identification with a "kinder, gentler" America.

The text contains only two illustrations, both of them black and white. Each text, whether short story or poem, has a set of questions called "Thinking It Over" and usually includes a word study as well. Teachers can assign the questions for oral answers in class, or they can assign them as written exercises, which is typical, and have students read aloud selected answers as part of a class recitation. Teachers often have the pupils read aloud the poems and short stories to check on their reading fluency in English and even on their ability to read interpretively. Andy's pupils use their own paper to answer the questions that he wants them to write out; but they also have their own workbooks for most graded exercises. Andy usually goes across[4] the "Thinking It Over" questions after his pupils have read aloud the text.

English Vocabulary

Most of the Amish parochial schools that I visited also used a series of vocabulary workbooks in every grade including the eighth grade. Entitled simply *Vocabulary Workbook*, this excellent series is published by Pathway. The forty-two lessons for grade eight involve word matching, use of the word in a sentence, and graphing of syllabic emphasis in pronunciation and correction of words that are intentionally misused in full sentences. As an example of the difficulty factor for this grade, the final lesson involves study of the words *anemone, attract, characteristic, chariot, dawdling, endorse, exhilarating, frivolous, furtive, habituate, luscious, pantaloons, permanent, perspective, rites, sagacity, shackles, symmetry, tortoise* and *tradition*. These fully bilingual children leave school after the eighth grade with a strong sense for the vocabulary of English.

English Spelling

The eighth-grade speller, *Learning to Spell*, was first developed in the 1950s by Ginn and Company for use in American public schools and is now reprinted with permission by the School Supply Room. The eighth-grade text includes some six hundred new words introduced twenty per week. The hardbound texts owned by the school include a thirty-page dictionary at the end and a set of pages addressed to the teacher involving methodology. The softbound workbook purchased by the pupil contains exercises with alphabetization, definition, synonyms, antonyms, and sentence formation using the spelling word. A favorite activity on late Friday afternoons in Andy's classroom is the vigorously contested spelldown which involves all sixth, seventh, and eighth graders standing around the periphery of their classroom at Baugo School while their smiling teacher stands at the back and calls out the words. Andy also loves to research and administer tiebreakers that are needed for virtually every spelling bee. He and I would often do this "work" together Friday at noon as we ate our lunch while the children were out on the playground. I remember this fondly, including one stumper from my own past, *antidisestablishmentarianism*, that caused about thirty raised eyebrows when it was called out.

History and Geography

History for the eighth grade at Baugo School uses a text published in 1995 by Pathway Publishers entitled *Glimpses of the Eastern Hemisphere*. After an introduction to map reading and to cultural history and geography of the entire planet, the text moves on to Europe, then Russia and the Commonwealth of Independent States, then Asia, followed by Africa, and finally Australia. The text has many maps of various kinds and photographs, all of which are in black and white, in keeping with the Amish interest in simplicity and earnest hard work where you learn without colored highlighting and outlines that someone else has made for you. This also saves printing expense for the publisher, and ultimately for the school that must purchase the text.

The text is very complete and up to date, including study of a reunited Germany and a collapsed former Soviet Union, now called the Commonwealth of Independent States. The workbook includes many map exercises, matching and fill-in exercises, work with an atlas and encyclopedia, and pronunciation guides. Andy has his

7.2 States Project in an Upper-Grade Classroom: the children, and any adult visitors, enjoy seeing what these upper graders have learned about states they would like to visit.

students do an additional atlas and encyclopedia exercise on the United States where each pupil chooses one state, makes a colorful map out of construction paper, and fills in the most significant features of the state. Andy laminates these projects and suspends them from the ceiling of the classroom for all to enjoy (plate 7.2).

Health

Health is also taught as an eighth-grade subject. Instructional Fair, a publisher for homeschooling, developed the text used at Baugo School, *The Human Body*, in 1990 as part of the Reproducible Activities series. This text gives instructors explicit permission to copy the worksheets for their pupils to fill out. At the end of the text is a series of the same worksheets with the correct answers that teachers can use for checking student work. Andy assigns approximately three pages per week for his pupils to research using the three sets of encyclopedias in his classroom library. Questions that the pupils cannot answer using these materials come up during the study period, and he discusses them with the entire class of eighth graders.

These materials must be tailored by the teacher to suit the special needs of the Amish schools. Several times I was asked to substitute on a Wednesday when health is taught. On one of those Wednesdays, I discussed my diabetes with the eighth graders, since that is a common health problem among the Amish. I explained how I must monitor my blood sugar, take my medication, and change my diet to keep it in check and avoid potentially frightful long-range consequences. At the very beginning of the eighth-grade health class that day, I charted my blood sugar for one month on the board. As I turned around, I saw that what had begun as an eighth-grade health lesson had become a sixth-, seventh-, and eighth-grade health lesson, since all thirty pairs of eyes were intently focused on me for my anecdotal lesson.

On another Wednesday, I forgot where I was, and simply started grading an exercise that Andy had assigned the week before, a lesson on the endocrine system. I had the pupils exchange papers (and I didn't even look at what they had in their hands—how could an experienced teacher commit such an error!); then I proceeded to read aloud from my answer sheet at the back of the book, looking up at each answer to be certain that they had no questions. No problems with pituitary gland, pineal gland, thyroid gland, adrenal glands, and pancreas. But then I continued to the next word, pronouncing it clearly, "Ovaries." And the room went deathly silent. I said, "Don't you have that?" and looked at Sharon, who was my guide for all questions of whether I was doing it right. She shook her head quietly in a very small way; I went to her side; she blushed as I took her paper. Clear for all to see was that Andy had blanked out the illustrations of ovaries and testes before he made his copies; they would not be discussed in this Amish classroom. No one said a word about it to me, not then, not the rest of the day. I don't even know if word got back to Andy, but I suspect it didn't because he has never mentioned it to me even though we enjoy kidding around with each other about many topics. I had just learned yet another lesson the hard way: Health in an Amish school does not include discussions of reproductive organs! Modesty is important to them; and the substitute teacher had been immodest.

German

Wednesday is also the day for teaching German at Baugo School.[5] The German reading text that this school uses for the sixth, seventh, and eighth grades is a dual language edition of the Bible, King James English on one page and Luther German on the facing page.[6] Students are assigned a portion of Scripture for study and for reading practice. During class, each person must recite clearly the verse that falls to them. Most of the work involves careful pronunciation of Luther German and memorization of certain well-known texts that are regularly used for prayer or for preaching in the biweekly service of their *Gemein* (the dialect word for Standard German *Gemeinde*, meaning church community). One teacher, whom I observed regularly, has his students complete challenging Bible quizzes that he has written in German.

Amish church leaders have been concerned for many years now about the decreasing ability of their church members to read and fully understand the difficult ecclesiastical language of Martin Luther's translation of the Bible, with its often tortuous sentence structures. Their home dialect, like all dialects of German, relies on short sentences and on common understandings of word usage that have changed radically over the course of five hundred years. Their home dialect was also changed during the two hundred years of their existence in America into a unique mixture of German and English not found in Luther's translation of the Bible. Most importantly, their home dialect of German is a spoken language, not a language in which one is literate. So the task of helping their children become literate in this German is very complex.[7]

The Pathway series on German provides a good start for this life-long learning task. The initial two texts in the Pathway series are a workbook *Let's Learn German* and a hardbound text *Let's Read German*. Most schools supplement these two texts with a writing and reading book *Erstes Deutsches Lesebuch*, first published for American schools in 1887 and now reprinted by Raber's Book Store in Baltic, Ohio. Learning to read German begins in the fourth grade at Baugo School by teaching the children to read the old German script, *Fraktur*. Most middle and upper grades have both an English alphabet and a Fraktur alphabet at the front of the classroom. The Fraktur alphabets at the front of Elizabeth's and also Andy's classrooms were hand lettered and then donated to the school by an older woman in the church district.

In the middle and upper grades many schools also use readers developed by Schoolaid. *Wir lesen Geschichten aus der heiligen Schrift* retells the most important Old and New Testament stories in a more straightforward form of German, with abbreviated sentences and less complex sentence structures than those found in Luther's translation. The hardbound text and included exercises stress reading comprehension above all. The last book in the Schoolaid series is entitled *Wir lesen und sprechen Deutsch*.

Andy's pupils use something else for their German work—a bilingual edition of the Bible. Using facing pages of King James English and Luther German, this edition subconsciously makes the point that King James English is to modern English as Luther German is to what Amish speak at home, namely, a lot different. Then, too, the bilingual edition is really helpful for glossing difficult terms and old language forms.[8] The hope is that more exposure to the most important text in their lives in both languages will spill over into their understanding and their ability to read at home and hear at church *die Luther-Bibel* with comprehension.

These seven subjects comprise the final curriculum for the eleven eighth graders enrolled at Baugo School. At the end of the school year, in early June, Andy, and his wife, Anna, prepare a lovely graduation ceremony for each of their eighth-grade classes.

Since graduation, two of the girls from the eighth-grade class I observed have gone on to work in businesses owned by their families, one a micro-industry for fine furniture and the other a home store. I hope that both will one day become teachers because they are such avid learners themselves. The best math student in the class, a young man, now does construction work, and with his bright active mind, I imagine he regularly comes up with "math stumpers" for his work crew. Their school life has turned toward work, and the practical preparation of their school days should serve them in good stead as they enter the adult world.

These young graduates of 1997 regularly meet now on Wednesday evenings for a singing and social time in another church member's basement. It is their bishop's way of keeping them in touch with one another and with him as they approach the time when they will join the church, marry, and have families of their own. Boys and girls sit across from one another at long tables with the ministers at both ends and the parents sitting on benches around the entire periphery of the room. Although the young people sit at the table, this is a family-invited function.

Chapter Eight
Teacher Education

One question that I often hear when I speak about the Amish schools is, "How can the Amish be adequate teachers when they don't even attend high school?" I understand why some who have received a college degree and have met the additional requirements for a teaching license might feel that an Amish teacher's preparation is so different from their own training as teachers that they find it inadequate. I am convinced, however, that the Amish teachers, whom I have observed during my own long career as a teacher, are competent and that some of them are truly gifted teachers.

The Amish attitude toward education must be understood from historical perspectives. When my grandparents went to school, people typically finished school with the eighth grade. This was the tradition of the one-room country school in the eighteenth and nineteenth centuries. By the twentieth century, a *secondary* school education was the norm. The Amish considered this "new" development worldly. If an eighth-grade education was good enough for their forefathers, it was good enough for them.[1] Contemporary Amish parents certainly would not want their children to leave school *before* the eighth grade. That has been the traditional time to leave school, and tradition is very important to them. But to then assume that Amish learning stops after the eighth grade is not to understand the Amish approach to life. Amish teachers speak often with their pupils about how important it is to continue one's learning after formal schooling has ended, and they bring in older Amish church members to reinforce this for their pupils. After graduation from school, learning continues—on the job—as it would in a skilled trade; and this same apprenticeship approach applies to learning to teach as well.

The *Regulations and Guidelines* encourage teachers to continue their education through obtaining a GED, not because of accreditation, but because a knowledge and skills base beyond that of one's pupils is always helpful. Some Amish teachers have studied for and received the GED, and I would expect that this option might be chosen more often as the number of life-long Amish teachers increases; but the simple fact is that such additional formal learning is no more important than one's sense that this is a calling and that one's pupils are a sacred trust. In that context, Amish teachers strive to perfect their knowledge and understanding constantly. They continue their education as they teach. They do so by using teacher's manuals written by master teachers, whose lesson plans they internalize as they teach. They do so by modeling the behavior of their former teachers, and that of teachers, whom they learn to know and respect as they teach. They do so by attending regional teachers' meetings where they are encouraged to ask questions and discuss problems.

Noah, as I will call him, has taught for over ten years now and devotes himself to this work. Noah defines the qualities of a teacher in the Amish schools thus: "You have to be an avid learner yourself; and you have to be able to see applications in everyday life for what your pupils are learning. You must have respect for other people; and you must have personal humility."[2] The latter two qualities that Noah emphasizes, respect and humility, explain why Amish teachers are truly open to correction. They believe that pride is harmful to one's soul. And the ultimate goal in life has nothing to do with worldly success; it has to do with moral and ethical decision making.[3] Accordingly, Amish teachers consistently evaluate the quality of their work, and of their life, and strive to improve. If what one is doing is not showing consistently good results, one tries to change, and that often involves turning to others whom one respects.

In a traditional, word-of-mouth community, people are being evaluated constantly, but not necessarily formally. Members of the school board do come to visit, as families, but they do not fill out a formal evaluation. And when grade cards are sent home every six weeks, families discuss how their children are learning, and how well the teacher is directing that learning.[4] In matters of evaluation, much is left to the discretion and understanding of the head teacher, in consultation with the school board, at the time when the needs of the next term are discussed.

Amish teachers who stand at the very beginning of their work have the greatest need for training resources. Beginning teachers have several excellent written sources of help as they begin their teaching. Three publications written by Amish schoolteachers and published by Pathway Publishers ($3.00 to $4.00 each) give well thought out descriptions of the personality of Amish schoolchildren, of special needs that young learners have, and advice on how to deal with discipline. *School Bells Ringing: A Manual for Amish Teachers and Parents*, written by one of the earliest Amish schoolteachers, Uria Byler, contains a wealth of practical advice for beginning teachers in its eighty pages. He discusses how to get ready for the first day, how to deal with tender young learners, and how to handle discipline in the first section of his book. The second section has specific suggestions for how to teach each of the major subject areas: reading, arithmetic, spelling, history, geography, English, German, and health. The third section presents very practical hints for matters that go beyond the curriculum. Here he discusses the PTA and other issues of working with parents, how to answer questions from children, whether to fail a child, how to use duplicators and copiers, assigning and checking homework, administering exams, filling out report cards, playing games at recess, among many other topics.

A second pamphlet for beginning teachers is entitled *Tips for Teachers: A Handbook for Amish Teachers*. Some eighty-six teachers contributed to the volume, including ten from Indiana. I have observed several teachers successfully using ideas from this practical, idea-packed, and inexpensive booklet. The first section of the first chapter, "Everyday Tips," contains fifty paragraph-long suggestions, including giving each child a set of folders—one for each subject—that will help them keep their homework orderly;[5] giving first graders clothespins colorfully labeled with their names for clipping their boots together;[6] having the children test their teacher for a change;[7] giving each student a stamped envelope addressed to their teacher and having them write the teacher a letter during summer vacation.[8] One teacher admonishes beginning colleagues to start a five-year diary "to keep track of what you're doing in school. Next year you can easily compare your progress in the books by glancing at your diary reports. Add amusing incidents, unusual happenings, visitors, etc., and you will have an interesting account of your teaching."[9] The second section of chapter one offers seventeen suggestions for drills in arithmetic and English at all grade levels. One of the arithmetic drills speaks directly to Noah's admonition that teachers look for practical applications:

> When your seventh and eighth graders are studying measurements, stimulate interest by letting the pupils take turns to make up a problem involving farm measurements. . . .
>
> The boys will enjoy measuring their corncrib and figuring out how much corn it will hold and how much it contains at the present time. Or have them measure the silo on the farm and using the number of head of livestock fed from it daily, figure out if the silage will all be fed when the cows return to pasture.[10]

This chapter also has suggestions for memorizing, for grading, and for how to work with a substitute. It concludes with a first-day quiz of twenty-four questions that provides a wealth of information about one's pupils: "What subject is hardest for you?" and "What do you think makes a good school?" and some laughs too "If a rooster weighs 7 pounds when he is standing on one leg, how much does he weigh when he is standing on two legs?"[11] Other chapters discuss discipline, the primary grades, extra projects, compositions, ideas for free periods, what to put on the bulletin boards, indoor and outdoor games, and things teachers can buy to enhance their work.[12] I think this inexpensive idea book would be an excellent aid for any first-year teacher. Certainly beginning teachers in Old Order Amish parochial schools find this to be a most helpful continuing education "workshop" for home study.

The third self-help text for beginners is *Teacher Talk*, a selection of articles published during the early years of *Blackboard Bulletin*. It is much more anecdotal in form because of its origin, and hence a bit less immediately practical. That is not to say that it is any less useful; however, its focus is on broader issues of pedagogy, on issues of educational psychology, classroom management, and teaching effectiveness, particularly with pupils whose primary language is German. These articles are for reading and reflection during periods when the beginning teacher has time for thinking and developing or refining an approach to teaching in general terms.

These three are probably the most used general books on how to teach in the Amish schools. But equally strong sources of immediate help are the excellent teacher's manuals that accompany the various textbooks used in the schools. We have discussed several of these resources, but it lies outside the purview of this book to fully explore these materials. I will discuss two manuals as representative tools for the teacher, one for teaching reading in the early grades and one for teaching seventh- and eighth-grade English.

Following work with a preprimer and a primer for reading, first graders in an Amish parochial school learn to read English using a two book series published by Pathway Publishers and entitled *Days Go By* and *More Days Go By*. The one hundred-page teacher's manual for these two texts is divided into two sections—one for each text—and gives suggestions for teaching each story and its accompanying workbook exercises. A specific lesson plan is presented for each of the forty-eight stories in the series. The lesson plan always follows this pattern: (1) the teacher helps the pupils complete the workbook page "Working with Words" as the first step, since it introduces new words that will be used in the story; (2) the teacher uses contextual clues (pictures) and directed questions to help the children determine the content before they read and to generate enthusiasm for the reading; (3) the teacher has the children read the story aloud; (4) the teacher asks directed questions to reinforce both the content and the moral/ethical lesson; and (5) the children complete the workbook pages "Thinking about the Story" and "Learning through Sounds" as a seatwork assignment. Teachers are not expected to generate any of the questions themselves; instead, the authors prepare a methodologically sound and complete set of questions and procedural steps for each lesson.

The introduction sets the philosophy for the series: "The stories have an Amish setting and relate true-to-life incidents which could happen to any Amish child. The teacher should help the pupils identify with the characters in the story, thus making learning to read an interesting, exciting experience."[13] Notice that the authors assume that pupils will find reading interesting and exciting if they can be shown how to identify with the characters. This is the educational psychology that undergirds the entire Pathway reading curriculum beginning in the first grade. And teachers are given specific pointers for each story about how they might achieve this goal with their pupils. I will cite a portion of the instructions to the teacher for the first story since it shows how carefully the authors prepare a teaching unit:

> Discuss the picture on page 5, asking the children what they think is about to happen. Does the picture show things boys or girls would play with? Does it look as if it were a nice day? Do the girls in your class like to play with the things they see in the picture? Do they ever have friends come to play with them? Tell the children that Susan and Levi are coming to play, and in order to find out what happened, they must turn the pages and read the story.[14]

These instructions, written in a conversational tone, pose five specific and fruitful questions for the beginning teacher, questions that clearly will draw the children into the story and help them identify with the characters. And the pupils learn to use contextual clues, such as pictures, in the very first lesson. Instead of using hundreds of words and complex formulas for establishing a methodological approach, these Amish authors approach the problem the Amish way, directly, with a specific application. And the beginning teacher soon learns how to craft a reading lesson by following the explicit written curriculum of a master teacher.

After the first reading selection, the authors of the teacher's manual prepare another lesson for the beginning teacher—a set of content questions that not only focus their attention on new words, but also look more deeply at the ethical/moral lessons to be learned in a reading where two girls disagree while playing with their dolls:

> Discuss with the children whether they think Rachel or Susan were in the wrong. Stress word [*sic*] and terms such as "Rachel was *selfish* with her doll," and "Susan lost her *temper* and said she was going home." Ask the children to look closely at the picture on page 14 for clues of what happened when the girls jumped up. (The chairs tipped over, and the dolls were thrown on the ground.) Also ask the children if they think Rachel and Susan are having a good time, and let them tell similar incidents of their own. Stress the lesson that sharing brings happiness.[15]

The three questions imbedded in these instructions and the admonition to have the pupils relate this reading directly to their own play will surely bring a deeper discussion of the lesson. A beginning teacher who carefully reads instructions like these cannot go very far astray, at least not pedagogically. Such lessons for living continue throughout the *Days Go By: Teacher's Manual*. In the second reader, pupils read a story about a first grader named Peter who forgets to remove his hat when he comes in from recess, and about Levi who wants to be the first one finished with his workbook and in his haste mistakenly colors a cow green. In these stories, featured in chapter five of this book, both boys' mistakes occasion some laughter in the schoolroom. The instructions to the teacher read:

> Whenever possible, take the opportunity to apply the lessons taught in these stories in real life. There are humorous incidents that take place in every classroom. Try to teach the children to laugh at their own mistakes by reminding them of what happened to Peter. By doing this, you are not only strengthening the character of the children, but also awakening a new interest in their reading.[16]

The workbook exercises also have complete instructions and an answer key for the teacher. For the prereading stage of the lesson, "Working with Words," teachers are told that most new stories contain six new words, but that the first story contains twelve. The teacher is reminded to write the new words on the board and to practice each with the pupils phonetically. Their attention is drawn to the prereading phonics text that they used earlier in the year if they need to refresh their approach. Teachers are also reminded that some words in English "must be taught and learned by sight. . . [and that] . . . other words . . . can not be recognized as rhyming words by their spelling, yet they do rhyme, such as *calf* and *laugh*."[17] Whenever new words are introduced, they are listed with thoughtful instructions for the teacher: "To add to the children's spoken vocabulary, always use each word in a sentence as you pronounce it. As much as possible, bring out the meaning of the word in your sentence. For example, 'Did your mother *wax* the floor? To *quit* doing something means to stop doing it,' etc."[18]

In the initial prereading exercise, first graders are taught how to follow directions. Amish primary teachers need only follow these instructions from their Pathway teacher's manual to begin the year successfully: "From the very beginning, the children's attention should be called to these directions. The teacher might call on certain pupils to read the directions aloud. Impress the idea that directions are to be *read and followed*. If this can be done in the first grade, much trouble can be avoided in later years."[19] Thus, the mentor teachers at Pathway Publishers not only give specific directions about how to use their materials in the classroom, but also how to prepare students early to work on their own by following written directions. This method works very well in the middle and upper grades if the primary teachers have adequately prepared their pupils to read directions and to follow them carefully, without having to check constantly with their teacher.

The writing texts used in many Indiana Amish parochial schools are from the Schoolaid language series entitled *Climbing to Good English*. The method, which I explored in chapters six and seven, is demonstrated in a series of annotated teacher's manuals. The manuals for grades one through four are each bound separately; the more extensive manuals for the upper grades combine the instructions for two grades in one volume (i.e., grades five and six in one spiral bound volume, and grades seven and eight in another). We will briefly investigate the kind of instructions given to teachers who work with the seventh and eighth grades. One lesson concerns proofreading and revision of paragraph-length essays.[20] The teacher's manual gives four sets of information: (1) the exact text that the students have in their edition, including the instructions; (2) the mark-up copy of each text with the correct proofreading symbol for each mistake highlighted; (3) the corrected text as it should read; and (4) a carefully thought-out statement to the teacher about how one might score the revised compositions that each student will be preparing as the next day's assignment. Particularly, this last admonition deserves our attention since it shows a mentoring master teacher at work. The suggestion is that the teacher grade for form, logical development, content, clarity, and use of notes and earlier drafts in rewriting. Teachers are urged to write encouraging comments on their student's papers; and they are told that a percentage score is not really appropriate for compositions, but that fairness in one's assessment is the goal. I am certain that any beginning teacher in the Amish parochial schools will benefit greatly from carefully following these mentoring steps to successful teaching of English composition. With such helpful teacher's manuals for each text, combining teaching philosophy with carefully drawn lesson plans and richly annotated answer sheets, a beginning teacher has clear and practical directions for each day's work in every subject. One could almost imagine that a mentor teacher were at one's side.

The anonymous authors of *Climbing to Good English* regularly address comments to the teacher about how to approach a lesson: "Before students begin this lesson, call them to class and go over Lesson 49 [on organizing notes prior to writing an essay]. Students cannot be expected to do this lesson satisfactorily until they understand Lesson 49. . . . See that students get plenty of time to do these composition lessons."[21] They also give a rationale for many of the teaching units, a brief statement that helps a teacher who may love math but not love English to understand the reason for learning a certain method. These comments may help the teacher to generate some enthusiasm (or at the least, some deeper understanding) for the knowledge that the pupils will gain. A case in point is the explanation to the teacher before the unit on using the outline form for study: "Using outline form for study is beneficial for the student because it helps him organize his thoughts and therefore understand the material better and remember it more clearly. If he learns this skill at school and acquires the habit of using it, he will find it comes in handy in many ways later in life. We would certainly recommend teachers to provide students with numerous outlining assignments as well as other kinds of written composition in subjects other than English."[22]

Where it seems advisable, these master English teacher/authors insert a quiz that the beginning teacher can use verbatim. The answer key is complete with the exception of those exercises where the answers will vary. This manual is so complete, and the accompanying instructions to the pupils are so carefully worded, that beginning teachers have an English curriculum in a book. This is also true for the social science texts from Pathway Publishers and Rod and Staff Publishers in Crockett, Kentucky, and for the arithmetic series by Beka Books. Beginning teachers will have a lot of extra reading to do during their first year, but they are fortunate to have such complete teacher's manuals for virtually every subject. I have seen the annotated teacher's manuals for public school English texts at this level, and I would say that the manuals from Schoolaid, for example, are every bit as comprehensive, but not as broad in their reach. They deal exclusively with how to teach grammar and writing (not with literature), and they model that teaching. They also know that their audience wishes to see applications of Christian, Anabaptist perspectives.

For experienced teachers, there are regular opportunities for continuing education. One of these is a monthly periodical, except for the summer months, entitled *Blackboard Bulletin*, a periodical written for Amish schoolteachers and for the parents of school pupils. Many Amish families subscribe to a group of three publications from Pathway Publishers—*Blackboard Bulletin*; *Family Life*; and *Young Companion* (for teenagers and young adults)—for the nominal price of $17.00 per year. All issues of *Blackboard Bulletin* contain at least one story for children, several poems, often about aspects of Christian belief, a Bible quiz called "The Puzzle Page," a question-and-answer feature called "From the Desk of Teacher Dave," letters to the editor, stories and poems written by schoolchildren in "Junior Jottings," and an article by the staff of the periodical entitled "Wrapping Up." Most of the articles are anecdotal, but always with the focus of a problem typical of schooling.

During the 1999 calendar year, there were ten issues of *Blackboard Bulletin*. The January 1999 issue, developed especially for children, contains nineteen anecdotes, mostly unsigned. The children—and their parents and teachers—hear about difficulties typical for school-age youngsters, such as cheating.

In the story "The Ugly Culprit," a jealous thirteen-year-old boy erases correct answers on a friend's math test and puts in incorrect answers while everyone else is out on the playground. Another story entitled "A Perfect Score" describes a seventh-grade girl who cheats on one answer of a vocabulary assignment, feels bad for two weeks, and finally confesses to her parents and her teacher. "The Cheater" is about a twelve-year-old boy who falsely accuses a classmate of dishonesty in reporting his grade on a spelling test. Finally, "Not a Shortcut" features several upper-grade boys who find out how to get hold of their teacher's answer key for arithmetic. They use it for several months. When their teacher finally asks what is going on, they confess, but by now have lost so much learning that they have to repeat seventh-grade arithmetic the following year.

A problem that Amish children deal with is to learn the kind of self image expected by the community. The story entitled "A Childhood Lesson" describes a first-grade girl who learns not to be selfish while her class does a treasure hunt. Another story, "Not a Ballplayer," describes the plight of an eight-year-old girl who is good at learning, but never gets chosen for the softball team. In "Martha's Notebook" a schoolgirl thinks her teacher's prize for completing a difficult map project is unworthy. When her teacher forgets to give her the notebook that she had won as a prize, she rues her uppity behavior.

Disobeying one's parents is a major sin in the Amish community, one that will have repercussions. "Erma and the Poison Ivy" describes a little girl who disobeys her mother, goes into a woods full of poison ivy to pick flowers, and has to get a shot from the doctor. The story "The Sunburned Boys" tells of three boys who get badly sunburned by swimming in the middle of the day against their mother's wise advice. Another problem that no one wants is stealing. In "Matthew's Money Problem," an eight-year-old picks up a coin off his grandmother's floor. He takes it home to put with the money he is saving for a new baseball glove.

An issue that confronts parents and their children and also has spillover effects at school is what happens to those who don't want to do their chores. The story "A Willing Worker" describes the plight of a young girl who grumbles when she has to pick peas. Haymaking is more fun (pea-picking is for little kids), but alas, she breaks her leg before she can even begin the "glamour job." Now, she wishes she could work—even at picking peas—instead of having to sit still while her leg heals. In another chore story ("A Lesson Well Learned"), a ten-year-old boy grumbles that his brother, who has a broken leg, doesn't do enough work. When his parents punish this behavior by making him spend a day as a boy with a broken leg, he learns how hard it is to miss out on everything. One additional story, "James and the Eggs," tells of a boy who puts off finishing his chores (gathering the eggs is a common task for young children). He gets caught, and his punishment is that he can't eat with the rest of the family. You will have noted that being excluded from activities with friends or family is a strong punishment. Amish families take great satisfaction in group activities (from quilting, to singings, to haying, to auctions, even to pea shelling).

Finally, all schoolchildren (and all family members) must also learn how to get along with other people. I have already described how one very fine teacher watched carefully, especially during recess, and interrupted clique formation (standing on the sidelines and pointing and laughing) by enticing the girls back into the game of tag. The story entitled "The Boys Who Were Different" describes a five-year-old boy who learns that he must make special accommodations for one of "God's special children," a Down's syndrome baby. "Peter's Discovery" features an eight-year-old who learns to play what his younger sisters want to play instead of trying to make them do what he wants to do. "Why Linda Was Grumpy" tells of a jealous ten-year-old who is rude to her nephew and nieces when they come to play. Her later regrets are punishment enough. Teasing animals also can lead to significant consequences, as we learn in "The Dog Who Didn't Forget." A ten-year-old boy taunts a nice, young dog and learns too late that you can ruin a nice dog by teasing it. One final delightful story was written by an eleven-year-old. It is entitled "I Want My Share." The anonymous boy author tells how all his goats wanted to get in on drinking a pail of sour milk after one started drinking it. He then makes the delightful shift to how he and his siblings wanted to get their share of a burnt cake after his dad said he wanted to eat it.

These stories from the January 1999 issue all contain a moral/ethical lesson or a lesson for living involving school or family life, the two poles of a child's existence. All of them are presented from a child's perspective. The other nine issues for 1999 present nearly all situations from the perspective of adults, primarily the teacher, although some articles focus more on parental questions or bring the viewpoint of the school board. From February through December of 1999, *Blackboard Bulletin* published some 216 pages of anecdotes, articles, or letters to the editor on a dozen general topics pertinent to teachers and 5 additional ones more pertinent to school board members or parents.

The discussions in *Blackboard Bulletin* show teachers (and parents and children) confronted with real world problems. Although they may define aspects of teaching philosophy, these anecdotes and articles also attempt to provide practical, realistic advice to teachers on how to change behavior and how to foster learning, one's own or that of one's pupils. All suggestions are offered in the context of Anabaptist belief and practice: humility; seriousness of purpose; adherence to principles of order; and submission of self to a community of believers.

In addition to such written materials there are regularly scheduled regional teachers' meetings that provide helpful sessions on specific topics and always set aside time for questions from the audience. One school is asked to plan and host the program, and the head teacher there plans the meeting and arranges for speakers while the school board takes care of refreshments. This rotates among the schools of a settlement. One teacher explains the value of such meetings:

> . . . teachers, board members, and parents gather to share ideas of how certain problems might be handled. It is also a source of encouragement for a teacher, and a time to give and take with ideas.[23]

In Indiana, teachers' meetings take place every six weeks during the school year and combine teachers from several settlements, for example, the Adams and Allen County settlements meet together, or the Elkhart-LaGrange settlement and Nappanee settlement meet together. Teachers from other settlements are always welcome, and sometimes constitute the program for the evening. Parents whose children attend the host school also attend the meeting and prepare the snacks for the social gathering that always follows the program. These meetings last three hours or more and take place on a school evening. There is always a special topic that is addressed, usually by a panel of teachers, but there is much time devoted to questions from the teachers in attendance.

The meeting begins around 7:00 P.M. Members of the local school board and parents set up the benches for the meeting. Earlier in the day the pupils who attend this school and their teachers thoroughly clean the school by washing the floor, the desktops, and all the windows. During the week before, the teachers have put up samples of the children's work, colorful drawings and other artwork (plate 7.2), essays that the children have written (plate 3.12), displays of current projects, etc. The teachers from other settlements arrive by hired van, usually a nine to twelve passenger van owned and driven by someone who regularly transports Amish people. Most times these drivers stay in their vans during the meeting, but some like to come in and enjoy the activities.

The teachers are directed to sit in a block in the middle of the schoolhouse. They often number twenty-five to thirty persons, from first-year teachers to some ready for retirement after thirty or more years. Surrounding them on all sides are at least as many observers—parents, school board members, and families from the district that is hosting the meeting. At the teacher's desk in front stands the head of the local school board who welcomes everyone to the meeting, makes any announcements the board wishes to make (at one meeting I attended, the state school board representative passed out copies of the revised *Regulations and Guidelines for Amish Parochial Schools of Indiana*), and then turns the program over to the head of the local program committee, usually one of the teachers at the host school.

If the program is a panel presentation, as it often is, the panel members are introduced where they sit at the teacher's desk. There are usually "get acquainted" exercises for the teachers, often a set of questions that each teacher must answer aloud. These questions are usually written on the blackboard—after all, this is a classroom. Questions that I have heard, and had to answer, include, after the obvious name and school affiliation: What is your favorite Bible verse? What do you like best about teaching? What do you like least? How long have you been teaching? After the group has gotten to know one another, we turn to the program.

As is true of any professional conference that I have attended for university professors, some discussants give very interesting presentations, and some talks are obtuse and boring. The first two qualities that Noah defined in the beginning of this chapter, avid learning and imaginative searching for applications, occasion lively discussions at these teachers' meetings, demonstrations, and workshops. Many discussions begin with a real classroom problem, and with the phrase, "What would you do if . . . ?" I have heard discussions of English grammar rules that would probably make even Daniel Webster scratch his head; and I have seen complex math problems—real brainteasers—put on the board and solved using a new method that caused the math lovers in the crowd to excitedly take paper and pencil in hand. Following statements by each of the panel members, the floor is open to questions or comments from the teachers and from the observers and continues until all have had their opportunity to query the participants. This session is usually quite lively and often provokes additional statements or questions.

Next the meeting turns to a series of questions that have been written out on pieces of paper and placed in a question box that is passed around to everyone at the beginning of the meeting. The "question box" method guarantees anonymity; it allows difficult problems to be discussed without personal embarrassment; and it precludes grandstanding.

The meeting ends officially when the head of the local school board invites everyone to stay for refreshments, often served in an adjoining classroom or in the school basement. These include coffee and various kinds of soda, potato chips, pretzels or popcorn, candy bars, and fruit that are in season. This is a noisy, delightful time to renew one's acquaintance with people who live at a distance; to ask a particular question about a school problem; and to generally enjoy a community gathering.

The support that these regional meetings give to teachers is very helpful. They have a chance to hear what other teachers are doing and perhaps find a new technique for use with their own pupils. They can ask difficult questions anonymously and get an answer from any number of experienced teachers. They develop a strong sense of community with other teachers who become their friends over the years, and to whom they can write about their own questions and experiences. And it gives them a night out, a chance to get away from the constant pile of homework papers to grade and lessons to prepare. Not all teachers attend these meetings; but I have enjoyed a number of six-weeks teachers' meetings throughout Indiana over the past twenty years, and they have all been very well attended.

There is also a large two-day meeting of all Indiana Amish schoolteachers, publicized every year in the May issue of *Blackboard Bulletin*. Similar meetings are held in other states. The Western School Meeting is often held in Iowa; and there are also annual meetings in Kentucky, Illinois, Michigan-Ontario, and Ohio. These yearly meetings take place during summer break, usually in July or August, and are often hosted at someone's farm or a local school. The meetings usually last two days; local families provide housing for the visitors. The attendees are told to bring a sack lunch for the first noon meal and that other meals will be served. The announcement also provides a detailed map of how to find the meeting place. These meetings are always well attended; in fact, one teacher friend considers it the highlight of the summer break.

Indiana Amish schoolteachers have many opportunities to continue their learning, some formal, others informal. I know several Amish teachers who have taken correspondence courses, and several who have taken or have contemplated taking a specific course in which they were interested at a local university. Their calling to be teachers involves them intimately with the most cherished and sacred trust of the Amish community: their children. Those whom I have observed take this calling seriously; and they often worry about how well they have taught the essentials and about the kind of environment their classroom provided for children in their formative years.

Chapter Nine
Difficulties at School

Like schools everywhere, the Amish parochial schools in Indiana must address difficulties inherent to a schooling environment. Some of these issues (fostering respectful behavior; dealing with cheating; punishment of serious offenses) will be recognizable to any teacher. Other difficulties, such as the issue of modernity in textbooks, are unique to the Amish schools. And finally, some issues like where and how to teach learning-disabled children involve questions that are being debated in American education at large.

The Amish approach to difficult issues is consistent: they avoid problems by anticipating them, and if they do occur, by dealing with the situation immediately. We will discuss here only those issues that could lead to problems in schools if they were not addressed. Foremost among them is how to handle discipline, specifically how to foster respectful behavior.

Respectful Behavior

Disrespect is not tolerated in Amish parochial schools, nor is it allowed in Amish homes. Children are taught using the Biblical imperative of the Ten Commandments that they are to respect their elders. And respect means to obey what a parent says, to do so with dispatch, not to talk back, and to generally keep quiet when adults are speaking. This attitude is also fostered in the schools, where the teacher acts as a parent in the old sense of *en loco parentis*.[1] And

9.1 Teen Commandments: strategically located right above the pencil sharpener, these delightfully thought-provoking sayings will stay with Andy's pupils long after they leave school.

many teachers remark that Amish schoolchildren are very easy to teach (whether in a public school setting or in their own parochial schools). Part of the reason for this is the fact that they work hard at their lessons during the school day (as if they were working at a job), and that they do so quietly and without much moving around —as they have been told. This is considered to be respectful behavior by children in a school setting.[2] One thoughtful Amish teacher put up a chart of "Teen Commandments" for his upper-grade pupils (plate 9.1) using a very tactful, mutually respectful and deeply religious teaching approach to "explain" why children should act respectfully—as his pupils do.

Therefore, disrespect is a potential issue of discipline that Amish teachers guard against, but for which they have support in their community life and in Scripture. Moreover, the direct approach of the Amish to any problem is to take care of it quickly, the same day if possible. From a public school perspective, we should understand that discipline in the Amish parochial schools does not involve the issue of open classroom disruption, which does not happen in the Amish school. In all my years of observation of the Amish school movement in Indiana, I have not seen or heard of one instance of classroom disruption in the sense that that term is used in a public school setting. I also have never seen an Amish pupil act disrespectful toward a teacher. Perhaps this stems from the deepened understanding of the term "discipline" that the Amish have from their Anabaptist religious heritage, where a life of discipline to the unwritten rules of the *Gemein*, the religious community, patterns one's choice of clothing, transportation, housing, and even one's employment as an adult. Thus, staying "in order" is a part of everyday life. We should also realize that more than thirty years of warnings in *Blackboard Bulletin* and other teacher resources about what happens when disrespect is allowed to spread have had an impact on this issue. Finally, we should note that Amish teachers and parents are really quite careful about distinguishing between youthful exuberance that sometimes results in boisterous behavior and the openly disrespectful behavior toward an adult that would call for immediate action.

Cheating

In schools where pupils complete most of their homework assignments during the school day when their teacher is in the room, there are few opportunities for cheating. If a textbook contains an answer key (as some arithmetic and English books do), teachers cut those pages out of the textbooks before they are distributed to the pupils. Thus, cheating would involve looking directly at someone else's paper, whispering answers to one another, working out a shorthand method for doing the same using hand signals, passing notes back and forth, or (in classrooms where it is allowed) asking to work with someone else on the assignment and using that as an opportunity to copy answers. All of the Amish teachers whom I have observed keep an "eagle eye" open for overt signs of disruption of any kind. Accordingly, a pupil who turns around to copy from the person behind or leans forward or toward the far-away next row would be very conspicuous. Hand signals are also soon noticed. And whispering is not allowed in the Amish classroom. This leaves one less easily monitored way for pupils to cheat: using opportunities to work together as an excuse to copy answers.

Some Amish teachers feel strongly that students must learn to work cooperatively with their classmates so that they will be able to do so effectively on the job once they have left school. A schoolroom activity that allows limited working together would be for classmates to help one another with an arithmetic assignment. Here is one example of how it works. The teacher assigns the work to be completed to the entire class of eighth graders. He or she then moves on to the seventh-grade arithmetic period. The eighth graders work individually for several minutes. Then, one of the eighth-grade boys, a quick learner in arithmetic, gets up from his seat near the front (without asking the teacher's explicit permission since he has his tacit permission as long as it is done quietly and without disruption). The eighth grader goes to stand beside a boy in the last seat, and they confer quietly about their answers to one of the geometry problems. Then the boy in front of them turns around in his seat and joins in the conference. Everything is done very quietly and without much movement or gesturing. They point to various places on the paper that they are questioning and in the book, particularly the formulas used and the arithmetic proof. After about two minutes, the boy standing returns quietly to his seat and the other boy soon turns around to his own paper. Since their books have no answer key, they use one another as a check on the work. These boys are all very good students in arithmetic; they enjoy doing even extra assignments, and their teacher is convinced that they truly benefit from such brief and quiet consultations. But I must emphasize that this attitude is not universal among Amish teachers, most of whom would say that being able to move around more freely in their classroom leads directly to cheating, that is copying answers from one another without working through and understanding the process.

In order to forestall direct copying among pupils, many Amish schools have very strict seating arrangements that virtually preclude interaction of the sort described above. First, the desks in these classrooms are either bolted to long boards in absolutely straight rows, or, if freestanding, they are kept in straight rows by the pupils at the direction of their teacher (see plate 1.4). Second, pupils are not allowed to leave their seats without the explicit approval of the teacher. Third, no one is allowed to turn around to the student who sits behind them or to lean toward the person in front or to the row on either side. This is another example of the Amish practice of avoiding problems by anticipating them and by removing the temptation.

Punishment of Serious Offenses

How to punish really serious offenses such as disrespect and cheating is a significant issue for Amish teachers and school boards and parents. They do not approach this issue lightly, and they have not taken a universal approach to punishment, as public schools have tried to do, preferring instead to leave such matters to the discretion of the teacher, serving the parents and the local school board.

One Amish teacher spoke of having had a cheating problem early in the school year. This teacher confronted the boys involved and gave them a stern but quiet and private "talking to." The problem cleared up immediately and did not repeat itself. As befits their lifestyle, Amish teachers believe in speaking plainly. And since most Amish are somewhat introverted, they are deeply embarrassed to be singled out in any way during school, even for positive events like birthdays. This aspect of personality alone would mean that the act probably would not be repeated, since that would lead to being "called down" in class. Furthermore, the ultimate punishment would be for the teacher to have a talk with the parents. This would involve the child not only being singled out at school, but also having punishment at home as well, for most Amish parents support their teachers on issues of discipline.

The rare occasions when stronger immediate discipline seems needful at school bring a larger question into the picture, however. Whether teachers (and schools) should allow spanking is an issue that is discussed regularly among the Amish, and there is no clear consensus about whether this kind of punishment should be doled out. What is clear is that if corporal punishment is ever administered, it must be done as a last resort, for serious offenses (like repeated instances of cheating or disrespect), and in a spirit of love.[3] It is also clear that some schools do not want teachers to do so under any circumstances. Teachers who give a deportment grade regularly use a low grade in this area as a means of last resort, for the grade card will be sent home every eight weeks for the parents' signature, and every part of that grade card is scrutinized by most parents.

Inappropriate Competition and Bad Feelings

A less significant problem is the kind of bad feelings that can get started among middle- and upper-grade pupils who are often quite vigorous in their pursuit of good grades. It sometimes happens that the person who has graded another's paper makes a judgment call and marks something wrong. Then both sides may "get huffy" about how the paper should be graded, and the teacher finds himself/herself in the midst of a dispute that requires the wisdom of Solomon and the speed of the lion of Judah. If pupils feel that their teacher is taking sides or is favoring one pupil over the others, and these feelings are taken home and discussed there (as they surely always are), then it is inevitable that the hard feelings will get passed on, and the teacher will receive a note or a visit from the parents.

The teachers whose work I have observed are very careful to make clear what their grading instructions are before the papers are passed out. In arithmetic grading, they will say, "Answers without labels are wrong." Before the class grades their English workbooks, the teacher will say, "If they have not linked the two parts of the predicate in their diagram, that is one mistake." Of course, such precision does not answer all questions beforehand, but it lessens the number of judgment calls that a teacher must make. And that, in turn, will cause fewer opportunities for what pupils might construe as favoritism.

Learning to Work Without Constant Feedback

Children in the primary grades must learn to become self-sufficient, so that they can get their homework done during the school day. That is to say, they must learn to work by themselves, to read the directions, to understand them, to follow them explicitly, and to get their work done by the assigned time—all without immediate attention from their teacher who has two or more grade levels and numerous subjects to teach. This is hard for young children, as it is for many of us adults. But many Amish schoolteachers get pretty cross with second- or third-grade pupils who have not yet learned to work independently. They will say (on a bad day), "Read this. What does it say? [The child reads the instructions aloud.] Do you understand what that means? [The child nods.] All right, then. Now, why didn't you do that in the first place without asking me?"

My observations and my work as a substitute cause me to think that this kind of dialog occurs for a legitimate reason, and that it has little to do with the crabby teacher syndrome. If the child does not internalize a sense for responsible behavior early in life, that same person as an adult will not be a self-starting worker, one who studies what needs to be accomplished and then goes about the task. If lazy habits continue for a length of time, they become deeply imbedded patterns of behavior. We must also remember that the Anabaptist religious heritage seeks adults who knowingly embrace obedience to God's will, as expressed in Scripture and interpreted by the religious community. If children do not learn to read and then do what is required, they will not be prepared to join the church as adults. Finally, Amish people are used to speaking plainly, telling the truth, as they see it, without subtlety and with few words. Thus, first- and second-grade teachers who seem to cut their pupils little slack on the issue of working for oneself and completing the task are striving to get their own work done, yes, but also to teach these children a deeper lesson of self-starting obedience. This can be a difficult task.

Learning Not to Speak Out

An issue that plagues primary teachers is pupils who haven't learned not to talk out. In the middle of a lesson a teacher will call out "Schtill!" and it gets suddenly quiet. In first grade, pupils must learn to raise their hand and be recognized by the teacher before they say anything. If they cannot do so, the first step that most teachers take is to pause and stare at the offender openly and firmly. For repeat offenses, the teacher will call the pupil by name and tell them to raise their hands; then he or she will make them wait patiently for a moment or two before they are recognized. Offhand, unrecognized comments, no matter how "cute" or interesting they may be, have no place in school. They disturb the general orderliness as much as crooked rows do in a planted field.[4] This certainly is an issue with which public schoolteachers also must deal, but in the Amish school, where several classes and a variety of subjects are under the direction of one teacher, quiet, self-paced work by each pupil is absolutely essential.

Another issue for the first several grades is sitting still and keeping one's eyes on one's own desk. Primary teachers may have to say, "Henry, I won't tell you again to turn around; that's the third time today I've told you to turn around!" The children do obey, when they are reminded of the rule. And eventually they do learn the rules that make Amish classrooms orderly places for learning and working: be silent unless called upon; sit still until recognized; work diligently until released—then you can rush outdoors, run and jump and work yourself into a sweat, and make as much noise as you want.

Unruly Behavior on the Playground

An offense that if left unattended could lead to more serious problems is unruly behavior on the playground. Amish teachers and Amish parents have little tolerance for unruly behavior. "Unruly" has to do with rules, and the Amish live their lives very effectively and happily with rules. School is to be a place of consistent, quiet, orderly work. Learning is not expected to be easy; it is work. And each pupil is expected to work to the best of her or his abilities, with self-discipline and with little direction other than that given orally to all and what is contained in the book. This attitude produces the kind of self-starting, hard-working, efficient, dependable worker that Amish people usually become.

Play happens on the playground. Recess means a break from the classroom and its rules; but for some few, it can also mean an opportunity for unruly behavior. Articles and anecdotes in *Blackboard Bulletin* repeatedly spell out the calamity that lurks at the school whose teacher does not go out with the children during recess because of the need to get a bit more grading done. This is the time when rowdiness may get out of hand among the boys and where cattiness may cause girls to form cliques that exclude certain other girls from games. Teachers are urged to play with their pupils during recess (and all of those whom I observed did so), to watch for evidence that someone is being excluded or pushed around, and to intervene immediately. Recess is a time for exuberant and even boisterous play, but it must happen within the context of the Anabaptist value system, which abhors name-calling and fighting.

Cliques

It seems antithetical to Amish Anabaptist belief and practice that the formation of cliques would even need to be addressed in schools. But human nature is human nature; and teachers soon learn that they must be especially vigilant about this possibly unseen virus. I call it a virus because it can soon spread. What might begin on the playground with a group of three or four girls standing on the sideline and laughing and pointing while others of their age are playing volleyball could very well end in the classroom with students who act snippy or uppity with other girls in their grade over grading practices or sharing songbooks. One of the behavior patterns most condemned by the community and roundly denounced in sermons is the sin of pride, called *Hochmut*. If several begin to think of themselves as better than others, very soon everyone in the room will be sorting themselves out according to what "group" they belong to. How is the problem addressed? Articles in *Blackboard Bulletin* call for strict vigilance; they admonish teachers not to let the children play alone at recess; and not to let anyone stand off by himself or herself and ridicule or pout.

Tension Involving the Amount of Work Sent Home

Amish children come from farm families where everyone is expected (and needed) to do productive work for the family. School-age children are put in charge of small animals, and/or help with cleaning tasks in the home, barn, or garden. By the time that they have reached their teen years, young people are capable of adding significantly to the pool of workers in a family. As more fathers must earn an income off the farm during the day, often not returning until after dark, it devolves upon the mother and the older children to do much of the farm work immediately after they return home from school. Children have little free time in the evening after school, and what they do have may be spent in community or family activities, like visiting people or going to money-raising events for the needy. Teachers, of course, view such events as very worthwhile, but they also know that some younger children need to spend more time learning such things as the multiplication tables and that older children may need time outside of school to write longer compositions or to solve more complex geometry problems. Whatever the reasons, there is some tension in parents between the desire that their children receive a solid schooling and the urge to put their considerable energy to use in providing for the welfare of the family. And carrying too many books home often raises the question among some parents of how much homework really is necessary. The parents who feel this is an issue usually visit the school and bring the question of the amount of homework assigned to the attention of the teacher.

Modernity in Textbooks

Modesty is a very important quality in Amish life. The Amish conceal more of the body with clothing than do those of us in mainstream American culture. Nowhere is that more evident than on a summer day when Amish families attend functions in public places. Plate 3.5 shows an Indiana Amish family at an auction and flea market in Shipshewana. An Amish mother may roll up the sleeves of her dress to the elbow, and that is her only concession to the heat of the day. Modesty involves covering most of the body, at all times. Men do not work without a shirt on the hottest summer day; nor do their children. Women do not work in their gardens or drive the hay bailer without a full dress and a scarf covering their head; nor do their children. Even in their own home all members of the family wear their long clothing, although some latitude is allowed young children. Under these limited circumstances, the youngest children may have some unfastened hooks and eyes; girls may wear a scarf or even go without any head covering; and babies may wear only a diaper in the heat of the summer. But that is in one's own home, not in public. Moreover, the choice of clothing is also limited. The Ordnung of one's community determines the colors of dresses and shirts allowed, and the fabrics must be without any print or lettering. All of these aspects of dress reflect Amish concerns for modesty. How does this affect the choice of textbooks for the Amish classroom?

Modern textbooks developed for the public schools in America are a riot of color. They are not serious-minded enough for Amish sensibilities. Reading and understanding involve serious-minded concentration on the word. Distractions like pictures, color highlighting, and boldly colored data windows distract the eye and the brain from the work of learning, from one's focus on the written word as a carrier of content. Accordingly, virtually all Amish-developed textbooks are in black and white, with few line illustrations. Secondly, they do not show people who are dressed immodestly. Dresses are long and they conceal the lines of the body; shirts are buttoned. But there are other aspects of modernity that are unacceptable in Amish society at large and certainly unwelcome in their schools, which train young souls who have not yet joined the church.

An aspect of modern life that the Amish seek to avoid is immodest topics of discussion. This means that all discussions of reproduction are avoided, as are discussions or portrayals of human reproductive organs. Teachers who use materials developed for homeschooling, procured from a source other than an Amish bookseller, must be very vigilant about materials they find on health topics. But this need for prescreening applies even to additional math story problem books or readers, because the illustrations used here might show inappropriate attire or use words that are rude or even blasphemous.

Then there are issues of income and greed and the "worship" of sports figures and entertainers. Many current textbooks attempt to entice pupils to learn by tying into their fantasy world in some "cute" or enticing way. Stories about enchantment or those that highlight sports stars or singers or models as a way to interest schoolchildren in reading more are simply not acceptable to the Old Order Amish, who attempt to live their lives apart from worldly influence, and whose only goal is to live life in a community that focuses on religious practice, in the hope that they and their children might go to heaven at the end of their days. No amount of wealth or prestige can buy one's way into heaven—and that is the goal of a life well lived. Accordingly, the reading materials that these impressionable young minds see in a safe school setting must be carefully screened by those adults who are responsible for their well being as if they were their parents.

Finally, even some subjects can be too worldly for some Amish parents. These include aspects of arithmetic that deal too prominently with speculative endeavors like insurance or the stock market. And many modern textbooks emphasize personal success and the acquisition of wealth, both of which are antithetical to Amish understandings of *Demut* (humility) and *Hochmut* (high-mindedness, self-aggrandizement, worldliness). Thus, when teachers decide to adopt a new textbook, they know that there will be significant discussion in the community about the appropriateness of the new materials.[5]

Teaching Learning Disabled Children

The Amish parochial schools in Indiana struggle with the many issues of working effectively with learning disabled pupils. Teachers in the Elkhart-LaGrange and Nappanee settlements have long worked with learning disabled pupils in their parochial schools, and they are being invited to regional teachers meetings in other Indiana settlements to discuss how they have implemented their response to these needs. I have observed this work directly in one school in the Elkhart-LaGrange settlement. In a school with three teachers, one is assigned to work with the learning disabled students in the large basement classroom. She has several pupils, each of whom is learning at a different level depending upon the subject matter. They join the other pupils upstairs for morning devotions and singing. Then they go downstairs while the other two teachers work with their classes. The teacher works with each learning disabled pupil individually, going over concepts with one and then assigning him or her a page in a workbook based on this material. They work together on several examples, and she then asks him or her to continue working while she moves on to the second pupil. The pupils work quietly and diligently. Since there are only three pupils for one teacher, she can see when each is stumbling and give assistance in a timely fashion. These pupils seem to be using the same materials as other Amish pupils, but are working several grade levels behind others their age.

In other schools where they have not yet implemented a settlement-wide plan for meeting these special needs, learning disabled pupils are seated with other pupils their approximate age, but usually near the teacher's desk so that they can receive help more directly. If the public school system offers assistance for several hours per week, the Amish teachers are very grateful and welcome this teacher into their school. Amish teachers in schools where such pupils must be mainstreamed admit to some frustration due to a lack of adequate time and preparation for dealing with these pupils' learning disabilities.

This discussion of difficulties in the Amish parochial schools will undoubtedly seem quite familiar to many readers who are teachers in other parochial schools or in public schools. Many of the issues are not unique to Amish schools; rather they are typical problems of the formative years of many children. As I write this chapter, a local television station is airing a news broadcast on the influence of a very young female entertainer on the dress and manners of preteen girls. One parent who was interviewed said, "We do not want you to *look* like her. We do not want you to *act* like her." There seems to be general agreement among the parents that this modeling is bad, and general agreement among the preteen girls that it was fine. As parents, we must all decide at what point our children are old enough to decide for themselves. Questions of maturation and self-actualization and models of behavior often cause problems, no matter where we live and learn. The Amish model of education seeks to surround the pupils with an environment that will allow them to succeed as Amish adults. That these schools are growing steadily in Indiana is a sign that they have been successful, even in the face of the inevitable difficulties of any human venture.

Chapter Ten
Community Interaction

As the school is the only building that an Amish community erects and supports with its time and money, the school occupies a central position in the community and is the focal point of many community events. Such gatherings as the Christmas and graduation programs attract virtually all members of the church community, as does the annual school fundraising auction. Even during the summer, schools are used on occasional weekends by fathers and children playing baseball or softball on the school lot.[1]

The school is also the place for typical Amish-Mennonite community relief work, serving as the collection point for a "sunshine box" of goods for a family who has great need because of some catastrophic event. One school set up its library as the drop-off point for such a sunshine box, a whole vanload of food, to help a family in a neighboring state whose father had been badly burned at work and was not yet able to return to his job. Another school had a huge barrel of aluminum can pop tops, which it was saving as part of a relief project to benefit people in the former Yugoslavia. School buildings are the most convenient and logical place for community outreach activities. Indeed, if we look closer, we will see the religious community vitally involved in the life of these schools.

The typical Amish school in Indiana is supported by one church district, comprising approximately twenty-five to thirty families or about 150–200 persons. Thus, although some events like the annual school auction do attract persons from neighboring church districts, it is more typical for an event at school to attract a full crowd the size of the district, and these events show us the value and support placed in these schools.

The PTA

Indiana Amish schools hold PTA meetings on a regular basis. In some cases oral announcements are made to the schoolchildren a few days before the meeting so that they can inform their parents. Other teachers send a note home with pupils announcing the date and time of the PTA meeting. Like the teachers' meetings, teachers often have their pupils wash the windows and the desktops on the day before the meeting, and virtually all have some colorful and interesting display of student work on the walls for the parents to see when they attend the meeting. Plate 7.2 shows an upper-grade display of state maps including geographical information and the student's choice of topical information about the state. Plate 3.12 shows a display of the writing of a classroom of middle-grade pupils. Parents arrive early in order to admire such displays.

The head of the school board is in charge of the meeting and brings up the items that need discussion, such as new textbooks that the teachers may be recommending, the cost of books generally, or work that needs to be done on the building and grounds— and introduces presentations on special topics.[2] Parents feel free to ask questions and to express opinions. One recent winter meeting dealt with the transportation of pupils to school, and especially how to deal with school closings. Since the Amish parochial school pupils are bussed to school in several settlements, and since the Amish do not have radio and TV for public service announcements about school closings, suggestions about how to get the news from non-Amish neighbors were greatly appreciated.

All such meetings have a time for refreshments and chatting after the meeting is dismissed. The school board designates families who will supply the refreshments: cookies, coffee, popcorn, fresh fruit in season, and soda that usually are spread out in a basement room of the school. Some schools use one of their PTA meetings as a teachers' meeting for all teachers from the settlement and from a settlement nearby.

Annual Workday

Just before the opening of school in August, most schools have a workday when members of the community come to the school to thoroughly clean the building, wash down the floors and desks, repair where needed, wash the windows, and paint the walls if that seems necessary. This annual upkeep is in addition to the daily and weekly cleaning that pupils and teachers do in their own classrooms. The strong sense of community in the church district makes such work an opportunity to take a break from other work and daily concerns and join with one's neighbors in community action and fellowship.

Annual Auction

This same sense of community action turns the annual school auction into an important event. Some schools rent tents to accommodate the crowds that such events draw (shown in plate 2.12). And for most events, the church district bench wagon is brought to school, and the benches are unloaded and set up in the schoolroom just prior to the meeting by those who arrive early.

A festive atmosphere greets those who attend, and that is part of the attraction in a farming community. By mid-afternoon everything is set up in and around the school. A portable grill for barbecued chicken is already smoking and the deep-fat fish fryer is ready as well; other food has been set up for sale in the school basement or under other tents. The auction includes quilts and other handcrafted items. Money collected from the sale of food and of items auctioned in the evening will be used for supporting the school during the coming year.

Such festive events are planned months in advance and word passes quickly through the entire settlement about which school is having an auction on what date. Auctions are always very well attended in the Amish community whether they benefit a school or a family whose medical bills have gone beyond their ability to pay using their own funds.[3]

Even Honeyville Elementary, the one public school in Indiana that teaches primarily Amish children, has such events. Their fundraiser, hosted by the Amish families whose children attend the school, is a summer chicken barbeque. This same school also hosts a potluck and volleyball game early in the school year, and a finger food and volleyball game later.[4]

Christmas Program

The annual Christmas program is a very special event for which the pupils and their teachers begin preparing weeks and even months in advance, for this will be the opportunity for each child to have a part in showing something they have learned to the entire community. To experience the Christmas program is to experience the deep sense of *Gemein*, of community, that forms the basis for their practice as Christians.

> Friday, December 19, 1997
> 10:30 A.M.–2:00 P.M.
> (program: 11:00 A.M.–1:30 P.M.)

When I arrive, the bench wagon is already sitting in front of Baugo School. The sixth-, seventh-, and eighth-grade class is just dismissing after having received their presents from their teacher—a gilded book which features a Christian poem or Bible saying in one corner, a beautiful nature scene, and the student's name in large calligraphy at the bottom. Andy and Anna made this present for each child—a project that I had seen spread out over their kitchen table several weeks earlier. The third-, fourth-, and fifth-grade class was still exchanging their gifts and eating a snack, so we couldn't set up the benches yet. After they were finished, several began pushing their desks and chairs over to the west wall, and the fathers and the school board chairman who had arrived went out to the bench wagon and opened up the back. Every two weeks, the bench wagon is driven to the house that will host the next preaching meeting, so that the benches and hymnals will be ready when they are needed. The bench wagon has a series of about five shelves on each side of the center onto which the benches are stacked. These shelves extend the entire length of the wagon since most of the benches are about twelve feet long. The benches have the name of the bishop written on the bottom side in the center. Each bench has a hinged leg assembly at each end. One man carries a bench into the school, flips it over, and another man usually holds one end, flips up the leg assembly, and then the two of them flip the bench over and move it into place. Occasionally, one man alone will accomplish this set up. The benches, about forty in number, are soon set up in rather tight rows extending from the wooden stage two-thirds of the way into the now adjoining classrooms. (Prior to my arrival, others had taken down the wall partitions that separate the two classrooms on the top floor to accommodate the large crowd.) Several benches also are set against the east sidewall. These provide seating for some of the women who have arrived early to help. People soon begin to be seated, as many more buggies have arrived by now.

In front of the stage, the teachers and their pupils have affixed a white sheet on a rope at each side. The head teacher and the middle-grade teacher will work the curtain from either side. When the program is ready to begin, they will pull the curtain part way shut. The room is decorated with state maps that the upper graders had made and suspended from the ceiling. In the middle of the room is a set of bells of various sizes made from cottage cheese cartons covered with tinfoil and decorated with red ribbon strands and red bows. The clappers are various sizes of pinecones. The largest group hangs from a string just in front of the teacher's desk. This arrangement of three is flanked on either side by a smaller grouping of two bells. On the east wall is the teacher's chart of the children's six-weeks grades, arranged from highest grade average down by grade level. Above this chart is a large statement that reads:

The Top Is Not So Important
The Important:[5]
To Apply Your Utmost Efforts
In All You Do

The other classroom on this top floor is decorated for Christmas, too. I do not go downstairs to the first- and second-grade room to see their decorations because of the need to set up the benches quickly, since the sixth, seventh, and eighth grade has already been dismissed and are out at the basketball courts or on the playground.

At about 11:00 A.M., the teacher in charge of the upper grades, and thus of the school, stands up and says in English that they are about ready to start the program, so would we please find our seats. I would estimate that there are about three hundred people in attendance. We are really packed on the benches at any rate. As new audience members arrive from time to time during the program, a man will indicate that a seat is free, and the person will work his or her way toward the empty place. At other times a father or a mother will get up and take a crying child or one who needs to be changed out of the room. One mother in front of me is feeding her baby carrots out of a baby food jar. When he doesn't want any more, she offers it to her three-year-old, who also refuses it. She finally eats the spoonful herself so that she can put the spoon into her bag.

The head teacher welcomes us to the program (most of which is given in English, but parts of which are in German). He says that we will begin with the first and second graders. Two boys come out to either side of center stage, standing back at the blackboard. Then one of them takes four steps forward, in a march-like cadence, and begins to recite in a very loud and clear voice a rhymed welcome to the program. He recites his few lines and is applauded loudly, and then it is time for the other boy. His bashfulness causes him to start while he is still leaning sideways up against the blackboard. His teacher, Manda, who is standing at the door leading to the stairwell and controlling the flow of students onto the stage, whispers his name sharply. He looks over at her, she gestures him forward, and he walks to the line marked on the stage floor and resumes his recitation in his very quiet voice. He seems to really enjoy the applause, or maybe it is just the relief that breaks out all over his face at the end. This class also puts on a rather elaborate skit with a table in the center and props on it that the children hold up and then say a memorized verse about the piece. Each class ends its part of the program by singing several songs. Among others, this class sings "Over the River and Through the Woods to Grandfather's House We Go." At the end of their singing, they file off the stage front left, down the aisle to the back of the other room, through their coat room and down the back stairs to the basement—all very quietly, while we all clap. Then it is time for the third, fourth, and fifth graders.

This class begins with a skit that is a favorite of every Christmas program: the recitation of the alphabet song in German. Each child holds up a card with two letters of the alphabet on it; the children line up so that we can see the entire alphabet, and then each child takes two quick steps forward, holds up the card, says the first letter and recites a German maxim linked to that letter, "M—*Morgen Stund hat Gold im Mund*," then says the second letter and its maxim, then takes two steps backward, at which point the next child begins. This class also does a skit that involves a typical class session in arithmetic. Sarah's Lavena plays the teacher. (Amish children often are known this way, as Sarah's daughter, Lavena.) She has her rather elaborate and very long part memorized. She speaks with the class of about six to eight pupils about learning to *use* their knowledge of arithmetic. She asks them how much money they would be saving during December if they began in January with one cent and doubled the amount they saved each month. After some guesses from the children that obviously don't please her (and a lot of silent guessing in the minds of those of us in the audience), she tells them to write the problem on the board, an old standby in the Amish classroom. One at a time the children go to the board, write up their month and do the calculation for their amount, while reciting it aloud (one, of course, makes an intentional mistake which triggers loud rumblings from the audience): January 1¢, February 2¢, March 4¢, April 8¢, May 16¢, June 32¢, July 64¢, August $1.28, September

$2.56, October $5.12, November $10.24, December $20.48. All of us are impressed with how much money we would be saving in December having started with only one cent. You can hear and see people expressing their amazement to one another.

This group also does another German skit in which they complete the phrase *"Ich bin dankbar für . . . "* One boy is judged to be too young to say what he is thankful for on stage. He is offended and says: *"Ich kann* doch *dankbar sein."* When they agree to let him say his part, he of course has trouble coming up with something and hems and haws around, finally settling on *"Ich bin dankbar für Wasser."* This precipitates a set of sayings on why we should be thankful for water, and makes the point very effectively that the simple gifts are often the most important. Following their skits this class also sings. The fifth graders line up at the blackboard, the fourth graders form a row in front of them, and the third graders line up as the front row. Among their numbers is a very nice rendition of "Stille Nacht." They then file off the stage, after some initial consternation on the part of some third graders about whether to exit to the back or to the front. From the side curtain, their teacher quickly sorts this out. Elizabeth whispers a name and makes a gesture toward the right direction.

Then it is time for the upper three grades. Following their presentation, they sing a set of songs, with the girls standing on the right and the boys on the left. The upper-grade girls are wearing white gauze aprons (like they would wear to special church services) over their dresses. Their songs include *"Herrlich, Herrlich Wird Es Einmal Sein,"* and they end with "We Wish You a Merry Christmas." Following their numbers, the curtains are closed and the head teacher says we should sing "Amazing Grace" while they get ready for the end of the program. Elmer's brother (a good singer, and one of those who often sets the hymn tune at church services) is sitting behind me. He keeps nudging me and telling me to "just start it," and since no one else does, I set the first verse as best I can, and everybody joins in. After we sing all four verses, we wait several more minutes, and then the curtains are pulled back with all of the children assembled on the stage to sing several songs. The head teacher introduces this by saying that it wouldn't be much longer and that he hopes it won't get too hot up here with ninety-four children on the stage. The last song that they sing is a surprise to all: "Happy Birthday to You." As they begin to sing, a group of children in the middle begin pushing an eighth-grade boy forward, and we soon learn from the song that it is Matthew. He is very embarrassed, but no one lets him step back from the front center until all three verses are completed: verse two, "Many More Birthdays to You," and verse three, "May the Good Lord Bless You." Everyone including the head teacher thinks the program is now over, but there are rumblings from the crowd; then someone whispers to the teacher the name of a member of the audience who also has a birthday. The song starts again, and as we sing an older man named John comes to the front to hear our congratulations expressed in song. This completes the program. All of the children file off the stage and the program is over. It is 1:30.

The head of the school board comes to the front and thanks us for our attendance and says that there are refreshments in the basement. We form a line to the basement Ping-Pong room where there is soda, coffee, chocolate milk, milk, oranges, candy bars, and a wide assortment of cookies, most of them homemade. Most take their treat and then go someplace to stand and chat where they won't be in the way of those who are waiting in line.

During the second part of the year, some schools also prepare an Easter program that celebrates the even deeper significance that they as Christians find in the Resurrection. The school is decorated with crosses and flowers made by the children and their teachers, and the program includes songs, stories, and messages about the Easter story.

Graduation

Formal schooling ends for Amish children with the eighth grade and a celebration on the last day of school in late May or early June. Once again the school is decorated for the celebration. At Baugo

With the compliments of your teachers
This Souvenir
is presented to you.
believing that it will find a place in your
Treasure Box.
and serve as a reminder
of our school associations.

Best wishes to your success.

Your teachers,

D

L

A

1996 - 1997

10.1 Graduation Announcement: a very special day in an Amish parochial school is commemorated in a very special way at this school.

School, the upper-grade teacher, Andy, and his wife, Anna, always make some memento of this occasion for the graduates to take with them when they leave school. One recent year he had found an old graduation card that had been used in his father's generation. He liked it so well that he and Anna reworked it for his eighth graders and took it to a local printer to be engraved. Plate 10.1 shows the announcement with names deleted for the sake of privacy. Every year Anna hand letters a diploma for each of the graduates, mounts it in a frame, and then surrounds the frame with a hand-made grape-vine wreath and intertwined silk flowers. On the last day of school, these diplomas hang from the blackboard when the pupils arrive. Attached to each diploma is a two-page letter from their teacher, Andy, who tells his pupils one last time of his high hopes for their lives; for the benefit of their presence in the community;

and of the need for life-long learning. The last day of school for the eighth grade begins, as usual, with singing. Then Andy reads them an inspirational text that he has chosen. He and Anna often make inspirational texts for his pupils and hang them where they will be read regularly, like the "Teen Commandments" that hang right above the pencil sharpener (shown in plate 9.1). Andy now dismisses the other two grades, and spends about a half hour speaking privately with the eighth grade one last time. Parents prepare and serve an early noon meal, sometimes a picnic. Eating together and telling stories about what school was like when parents and grandparents were young is a lesson in oral history. If the weather is good, some schools have a baseball or softball game between fathers and schoolchildren on the last day of school. Such games are played with great enthusiasm by young and old; and it is not uncommon for an old outfielder to have to hoof it into a real cornfield and spend some time finding the ball before play can resume.

Impromptu Family Visits

Teachers often say that they wish they would have more visitors at school. I have heard this comment in nearly every Amish school in Indiana. And it stands in marked contrast to the isolation of teachers and pupils in many public schools where visitors are directed immediately to the principal's office. Visitors to an Amish school will find no principal's office, indeed no offices at all. Instead, they will find teachers busy teaching, but not too busy to notice the visitors and to get a bench for them to sit on in the back of the room.

The visitors are often a mother and her preschool-age children. She will hold the baby on her lap, but younger children who can walk will often stroll up to an older sibling sitting in the class, where they will sit quietly on their sister's or brother's lap and watch what happens as the lesson continues. Babies, too, are often picked up and held by a member of the class, making it clear that this is a family school.

At noon, it is not an uncommon experience for a van to pull up into the school parking lot and a father or older brother who is taking his noon break to come in and say "hi" to everyone and to pass on a message to a younger sibling. Other visitors include older couples who have grandchildren in the school, and who have more time free for visiting.

All visitors are encouraged to stay awhile and bless the school with their presence. This often includes an invitation to say how they find the school or to say what school was like when they attended. The children turn around in their seats and listen attentively as these parents, grandparents, aunts, and uncles speak briefly about school now and in earlier times. Most schools have a treasured guest book for them to sign and perhaps to write a comment about what they observed.

Englischer Visitors

Some teachers like to arrange visits from people who are not members of the local Amish community. The community name for those who are not Amish is *Englischer*, their German designation for someone who speaks English. One teacher has invited his neighbor, a member of the Indiana State Police, to show the children his police dog and to talk with them about his work and about safety issues. This same teacher invited another friend who plays the bagpipes to entertain the children with hymns and other songs played on this ancient instrument.

Birthday Surprises

One morning you walk into school and see a note written on the blackboard, "Tomorrow bring a spoon and plate for noon." Everyone knows that that means a special meal catered by someone's mother, and dad, grandmother, or aunt as a special birthday treat for the entire school. This is a big production, particularly in a school of over one hundred pupils with no cafeteria, no refrigerators, and no electric stoves.

Buggies begin arriving about 10:30 A.M. and soon you hear bustling around in the Ping-Pong room downstairs as someone's family begins setting out the surprise meal. And what a treat it is. Teachers dismiss their classes one room at a time; everyone stands in a long line stretching down the stairs and into the lower room where the Ping-Pong tables are full of mouth watering food: Amish wilted salad, potato salad, baked beans, potato chips, fried chicken or hot dogs with garnish, and two liter bottles of various kinds of soda. Everyone serves themselves on their plates (or on one of the extra plates ready for those who forgot their own) and files back to the classroom where they eat with gusto. And you have already seen what awaits them for dessert after they have finished their meal—ice cream in five-gallon buckets, homemade cookies, chocolate cake or brownies!

After everyone has finished, the children are dismissed for noon recess. The teachers often open up the doors or curtains that separate the classrooms and push some of the chairs to one side to make an impromptu stage for an all-school assembly. When the bell rings everyone files into the larger room and gets ready to sing for the visitors who by now have put everything away and are seated at the front of the room on a bench. Each classroom sings a few favorite songs (nearly always religious in nature). The children may file to the back to form a choir facing their visitors and schoolmates. The last song is usually "Happy Birthday to You," which always includes the typical Amish last verse "May the Good Lord Bless You" sung to the same tune.

For some this may be the first time to learn who the birthday child is, for true to Amish values of modesty, the note on the board was not signed and no announcement was ever made that would draw attention to whose birthday it was. Indeed, other birthdays celebrated less elaborately will find the birthday boy or girl treating classmates before school by placing several sweet treats, gum, small candy bars, or pieces of candy on each person's desk from a large paper bag. Children will say "thank you" as the treats are placed on the desk, but no other overt attention is drawn to the birthday child.

Emergencies

It is the middle of a weekday night in springtime; torrential rains have already flooded nearby fields, and the members of the local Amish school board know that their school, which lies in a low field itself and has a basement, will be a likely site for flooding. Sure enough, the first- and second-grade room in the basement is flooded and water continues to pour in. Immediate action is necessary. I know nothing of this since I live nearly fifteen miles from the school where I have been observing for over a month. When I arrive at my customary time, 7:45 A.M., I find the school a beehive of activity. A gasoline powered trash pump has already been set up outside one basement room and is pumping away water at a tremendous rate. Men and women are carrying school desks from the basement classroom up to the vestibule where they are wiped down and then carried on up to the classroom which normally houses the third, fourth, and fifth grade.[6] Meanwhile other parents are setting out wet library books from the lower-grade room to dry, salvaging what they can. Still others are mopping up and cleaning the concrete floor and lower walls. This work continues for the parent volunteers for much of the morning in the basement, while the pupils and their teachers go about their usual business upstairs. By the next day, school is open again for normal business, thanks to the efforts of parents who worked late into the night.

At another school one wintry day when the temperature was hovering at one degree, the water pipes froze as the last children were arriving at school, most of them delivered by their parents in buggies so that they wouldn't have to walk in the raw wind. Rather than to dismiss school, some of the fathers went to the basement, and set about thawing and repairing the burst pipes, while the teachers started the school day with the children. In due time, the water was running again, and the fathers could get on with their other work, as usual.[7]

Community interaction with the school has strong undertones of religious practice as the two are linked by the Amish concept of

Gemein. Indeed, the Amish stress the centrality of religious practice to all of life. They do not distinguish between belief and practice, everyday experience and religious experience, religion and work. Their approach to the school and its work is a lesson for their children: schooling and religious practice are one and the same, just as community and the faith community are inextricably linked.[8]

Conclusion

Indiana Amish Schools at the Dawn of the Twenty-First Century

The Amish parochial school movement in Indiana continues to grow. In the Allen County settlement one large new school was opened for the 1999–2000 school year and another was finished in 2002; in the Elkhart-LaGrange settlement four new schools were opened in 2000; in Adams County three new schools were opened in the school year that ended in the spring of 2000.[1] Such regular growth in the number of Amish parochial schools reflects the pattern of growth found in other Amish settlements tracked by the publishers of *Blackboard Bulletin*, through the careful work of David Luthy, the foremost historian among the Amish. For the 1999–2000 school year, some 1162 Amish parochial schools are listed for the United States and the province of Ontario in Canada, teaching 32,193 pupils.[2] This reflects a growth rate from the previous year of fifty-two schools (a 5 percent growth rate) and 2053 pupils (a 6 percent growth rate).[3] For the 2000–01 school year, the directory lists 1188 Amish schools and 32,432 pupils, a growth of 26 schools (3 percent) and 239 pupils (1 percent).[4] Indiana's growth over 1998, was four schools (3 percent) and 424 pupils (8 percent).[5] And in 2000–01, Indiana listed two schools more than in 1999 (2 percent) and a slight enrollment gain of ninety-five pupils (2 percent).[6] These figures suggest continued vitality in the Amish parochial schools in future years.

Given such growth, finding adequate numbers of long-term teachers may become an increasing problem. The remuneration and the status of teachers in the community have risen. Men are also considering this profession in increasing numbers, but most schools still employ predominantly young, unmarried women, who teach for several years, and then marry and settle down to rear their own children. Thus, schools must deal with a rather constant change in teachers and with the more significant problem of lack of experience among the new teachers. Those of us who love to teach know that four or five years of actual experience are necessary even for the most gifted teacher to reach a comfort level that allows one to look ahead and anticipate problems; to have some longer-term perspective on the problems of the moment; and to be relaxed enough that one can begin to deal with learning situations intuitively, instead of always having to rely on a scripted workday. Amish communities will need to find ways to increase the pay of teachers, perhaps by adopting community-wide assessments (as at least one school has done) rather than to assess only parents whose children are actually attending the school. This leads us to consider what issues the Amish parochial schools are working to address.

Costly Schools

Many Amish parents, like so many American farm families, have only limited disposable income. The families are large; and although mothers strive to produce income at home, it sometimes is difficult to make ends meet. This is particularly true where three or four children are enrolled in the Amish parochial school: "teacher money" must be sent every month, and student workbooks and supplies purchased at the beginning of each year.[7] For this reason, schoolteachers who adopt new texts, particularly those that are disposable, realize that they are adding a rather significant burden to the budget of many families that attend their schools.

Some Amish parents send their children to the "free" public schools because of the question of cost. Yet others send their children to public schools to give them "a good head start." In some instances this includes just kindergarten, which Amish schools do not offer, and grades one and two, where the basic reading skills are set. Other parents choose to send their children to the public schools through the fourth grade. Then, because of worry about too much worldliness, rampant immodesty among preteens in public school settings, and similar concerns, these same parents want to send their children to Amish parochial schools for the remainder of their time in school. Some Amish school boards will not allow these pupils to transfer to their schools.[8] They worry that Amish children who have spent so many formative years in the public schools will bring worldly influences with them to the Amish schools and that they will be undisciplined and headstrong, even disrespectful, both in the classroom and on the playground.

Another cost issue is the need to continuously build new schools. Success brings with it the problems of greater enrollment. Even with donated labor and land, new schools are a costly venture. And many of the oldest schools in Indiana are now forty to fifty years old. These old school buildings must now be totally remodeled or even torn down and rebuilt. And Amish schools do not receive property tax revenues.

These are not new questions; and they also touch many non-Amish families whose children attend private schools or parochial schools of their affiliation. There is always a significant cost/benefit discussion in families whose children might attend parochial (or private) schools. Parochial schools derive virtually all of their support from their patrons; and this makes questions of fundraising, paying the bills, and the accordant benefits of this sacrifice a significant focus of attention. A related issue is the ability to keep good teachers, given the low salary.

Hiring and Keeping
Experienced Teachers and Substitutes

As teaching in the Indiana Amish parochial schools is considered by most teachers to be their real calling, one does not seek out employment here by filling out a resume and going to a central administrative office for a job interview; instead, the school board comes to you and asks you to consider teaching for a term, and they do so because they know you. They know where you live; they know what your belief system is; and they know what your general repute is in the community. This work is certainly a calling, but like so many service opportunities, the pay is not sufficient to support oneself alone and certainly not to support a family. Accordingly, it is difficult to keep full-time teachers more than a few years.

Another problem is finding persons in the community who can substitute when the teacher must be away for a day or so. Often there are retired Amish parochial teachers living in the settlement who help out occasionally, but it is not uncommon for them to live at some distance from the school where they are needed, and they must either plan for long travel times in a buggy or arrange for other transportation to the school.

Substitutes sometimes are drawn from outside the Amish community; and occasionally these substitutes become full-time teachers for a period of time, as did my grandfather. At least one school in the Elkhart-LaGrange settlement employed a non-Amish person full time as a teacher during 1996–97. Non-Amish teachers are often members of other Anabaptist churches, Mennonite or Brethren, and are known in the small community for their belief and practice as Christians.

But these substitutes have not attended Amish parochial schools, and they have not grown up Amish. Accordingly, they have a lot to learn; and the school board, parents, and pupils may also have a high learning curve for awhile. Even if one is well prepared pedagogically and in terms of temperament and even belief and practice, the first time that one substitutes in an Amish parochial school, one must do things in unaccustomed ways. Even more importantly one must *not* do some things that are habitual from one's training.[9]

The search for substitutes and for teachers is continual. Long-term teachers carefully watch for interest among their upper-grade pupils, and occasionally have them help out by teaching a unit to a lower grade. For some Amish parochial school boards, it is a yearly task to seek out and employ yet another new teacher. The word gets around at regional teachers' meetings, and some teachers are even hired away from one Amish parochial school to another—often because the new school is closer to home.

The Old Order Amish view their children as "an heritage of the Lord."[10] This understanding has caused them, among other things, to establish several successful publishing houses, a distribution network for their textbooks, a periodical on teaching, a program of continuing education for their teachers, a system of teaching and learning that requires no administrators, and a network of small learning centers that are truly community schools. This is a remarkable accomplishment in a fifty-year span. It reflects their belief that they are to be good stewards of what they have been given by God.

Amish parents and teachers openly express their thanks that they live in a country whose founding fathers were men of religion and freedom, men who believed that together we could create a better life for all, through education, and that the freedom to practice one's religion should not be regulated by the state. Abraham Lincoln, one of the finest and most honored graduates of the one-room schools of Illinois and Indiana, who wrote the Emancipation Proclamation and the Gettysburg Address, spoke these words at one of his last public addresses:

> With malice toward none; with charity for all; with firmness
> in the right, as God gives us to see the right, let us strive on to
> finish the work we are in; to bind up the nation's wounds, . . .
> to do all which may achieve and cherish a just and lasting
> peace among ourselves, and with all nations.
> Second Inaugural Address
> March 4, 1865

Old Order Amish teachers, pupils, and parents have established and work diligently to support with their time and their wealth a network of parochial schools in Indiana that fosters knowledge and morality in the context of their peace-loving religious community. I thank them for teaching me how to value another approach to learning, believing, and living.

Appendix
Report: A Typical Day in an Indiana Amish Parochial School

This report attempts to portray a typical day in a single classroom, focusing on a teacher of the upper grades as he does his work. The format for the day is typical of all normal teaching days in this teacher's classroom. The amount of time devoted to one subject or another differs from one teacher to the next and certainly among grade levels, but the variation is not extreme.

The sections on specific subjects (devotions, math, English, reading) are drawn from several days' experiences in January and early February 1997. In part, this composite was necessitated by our having had incomplete school days due to snow delays and due to in-service training sessions scheduled by the public school system, which supplies transportation for this Amish school. In part, it was occasioned by my notes being more complete for a given subject on one day rather than on another. In every case, the teacher's presentation of a given subject derived from a single teaching day and covered his teaching of that subject to all three grades. Specifically, the section entitled "Devotions" is my transcript from Tuesday, January 14; "Math" is the transcript from Thursday, January 9; "English" details the lesson completed on Thursday, January 23; and "Reading" is a transcript of work done on Thursday, February 6,

1997. I chose a composite approach because it allowed me to show aspects of teaching and learning that offer virtually a verbatim transcript.

7:45–8:15   TEACHERS ARRIVE

Two of the teachers arrive by buggy; one who lives several miles away has a driver and arrives by car. The teacher for the upper grades stables his horse in the barn adjacent to the school. He also starts the generator and water pump and then enters the school building, goes through his classroom, and hangs his hat and coat at the left end of the coat rack at the front. He sets his lunch container (a small cooler) on the top shelf and places his thermos of coffee on the floor beside his desk. He lights the gas lamp beside his desk. Then he checks the coal stove at the back of the room, shakes down the ashes, and has a seventh-grade boy, who walks to school and had arrived early, take them out to the ash pile behind the school while another gets a bucket of coal. (This school used about five tons of coal in the winter of 1997 at a cost of $140 per ton.) He goes to the blackboard and writes the assignments in math and English on the board at the front of the room (eighth on the left side, seventh in the middle, sixth on the right). He draws several solid geometry figures on the board at the eighth-grade end (cone, triangle, pyramid). In the middle of the blackboard at the top he writes a maxim that will draw pupils' attention to moral/ethical questions or make them chuckle ("Learning Dispensed Here Free of Charge/ Bring Your Own Container"). Having done his early chores, he sits down at the comfortable secretarial chair behind his spacious oak desk (built by an Amish cabinet maker from the district in which the school is located), and arranges arithmetic and English papers that are to be handed back according to the seating order in his classroom. He checks the *Teacher's Weekly Schedule* book to be certain that all assignments are worked out and that the pages to be graded and those to be introduced are listed. By 8:00 some children have already arrived (those few who walk or come by buggy); some have questions about their homework. He says a friendly, "Good Morning," as others come in. Three fourth-grade boys get the basketball pump out of his lower desk drawer to pump up their ball. He tells them where the snow shovel is so that they can shovel off their court.

8:20   BUSSES ARRIVE

Most children at this school arrive on two busses provided by a county public school corporation that transports the Amish school children after they deliver those who attend public school. As soon as they arrive, most of the boys go out to play basketball while some of the girls go to the basement to play Ping-Pong. Others stand and talk together or work out their arithmetic, English, or reading homework in small groups at someone's desk.

8:45   BELL

The teacher picks up the little bell on his desk, walks to the back door, and rings the bell several times for the boys playing basketball outdoors and once in the back stairwell for the girls and boys who are playing Ping-Pong in the south basement room. The children come in quickly and need about three minutes to take off their wraps and hang them in the closet at the front of the room. Some of the boys comb their hair (from the middle to the sides) at their desks. The girls, who pull their hair back to the sides under their white gauze Kapp, do so in the cloakroom. The girls use the right end of the coat closet and the boys use the left. There is some good-natured jostling of each other in the closet before they come out and quietly take their seats.

8:50   PRAYER

All thirty-one students wait quietly in their seats until the teacher stands and says, "Let's bow our heads in prayer." All stand, fold their hands, and bow their heads, and the school day begins with the Lord's Prayer recited in German quickly from memory by one of the seventh-grade girls whose turn it is today—they follow a regular rotation through all the pupils in the classroom. They sit down following the prayer, and again wait quietly and attentively until the teacher determines what they will do next.

8:51–9:30   DEVOTIONS

The teacher says simply, "Let's sing some songs today." Immediately the eighth-grade boys get up, collect the blue *Country Gospel Hymnbook II* and the small black *Unparteiische Lieder* from the bookcase at the back of the room, and pass them out to the others as they come to stand in their proper place at the back of the room in front of the wood panels that separate this room from the middle-grade room—its mirror image on the North. The girls stand on the right side with eighth in the back, then seventh, and sixth-grade girls in the front; and the boys reiterate this arrangement on the left side. The teacher stands in front of the group and says, "Number fifty. John, do you want to start it? Let's try the first four verses."

> We are living, surely living, in the days he speaks about,
> All of these we now are having every day;
> Let's be ready for His coming, let us meet him with a shout,
> For He tells us in His words, to watch and pray.

The tune is set by John who sings a word or two, at which point all the rest join in at the pitch, which he has set. (Later songs are set by girls and also by the teacher.) The singing is loud, but controlled. Most songs are sung in unison; but several favorites have a descant sung by the girls or the boys, or are sung in the form of a round. The six songs take nearly forty minutes to sing. While singing, many of the children have a fixed expression on their faces. Girls often stand with one hand encircling their waist and the other holding the book; boys stand with most of their weight on one leg or the other, and put a hand on one hip. At the end of the singing, virtually all of the boys quickly go out to the entranceway to get a drink of water, while the girls go immediately to their seats. All are in their seats again and sitting quietly within two or three minutes.

9:30–10:35   MATH

The teacher says, "We'll start with eighth-grade math. Is everybody done?" Before he begins the grading, the teacher takes several minutes to talk with each of three eighth graders who have raised their hands to ask him a question.

Each subject period is subdivided into work done by each grade level. And within that grade level the teacher always proceeds from grading, to taking down the grades, to introducing the new assignment. While the teacher works with one grade level the other two are finishing their homework in this subject or are working on an assignment in some other subject. If they are interested in what is being done by another class—or if the teacher begins to tell an anecdote—they will listen intently before returning to their own work. Those very few who have finished all their assignments are allowed to read a book that they have purchased or have checked out from the public library branch located about a mile from the school.

Eighth Grade [about 25 minutes]

The teacher says, "Okay. Exchange your papers." The person at the back brings her paper to the front and all the others hand their paper to the person sitting behind them. "Page 375, number one is 37 and 5/7th square inches. Number two, $39.60 and $60.34. Number three, ninety square inches, etc." He reads off the answers very quickly from his answer pages (which have been cut out of the student texts, effectively removing any temptation). This takes only two minutes for a three-page assignment. Accordingly, the students must listen very attentively. A few students raise their hands to have him repeat an answer. Then he returns to his desk, takes a pen, his Long Ranger EZ-Grader, and his grade book (which is always open on his desk for the students to look at during recess, and which remains at school on his desk overnight), and simply says, "Anna?" and Anna gives the number which she missed, "One." He says, "Ninety-eight." After he has started the process with several students, the others call out their scores in the alphabetical order of their entry in his grade book, automatically and quickly, without his needing to call a name. (The pupils are not seated alphabetically, but they know the usual order of their teacher's grade book; they also know that he won't call their name aloud—potentially embarrassing—if they beat him to it.) This whole process of grading, from giving the answers to entering the grades often takes no more than three or four minutes. Following grading is the explanation of the

work for Tuesday. The teacher says, "Okay. Page 378 is measurements to remember. Put them in your [memory] bank." He reads
the instructions directly from the book:

THE VOLUME OF A PYRAMID

The solid shown here is a *pyramid*. The sides of a pyramid
are all triangles. Its base may be a triangle, a rectangle, or a figure of some other shape.

The point *A* is the *vertex*. The line *AB*, which is perpendicu-
lar to the base, shows the *height* of the pyramid.

Take a hollow prism and a pyramid, each having the same
base and the same height. Fill the pyramid with sand and pour
the sand into the prism. The contents of the pyramid will fill
exactly 1/3 of the prism; hence the volume of the pyramid is
1/3 of the volume of the prism. But the volume of a prism
equals the area of the base times the height; hence

Volume of pyramid=1/3 x area of base x height,
or V=1/3Bh

(Strayer-Upton,
Practical Arithmetics Book Three, 378)

Before school the teacher had drawn a pyramid on the board and
the formulas for figuring both the volume of the pyramid and the
surface area of the figure. He walks to the board, points to the figure, and says, "Volume equals one third," points to the base and
says, "the *area* of the base," and points to the height and says,
"times the height." He continues, "In problem one, the area of the
base is six square inches and the height is five inches. What would
the volume be?" He waits until about half the hands are in the air,
and then he says, "Noah." When Noah answers, "Ten," he asks
what the unit is; and when Noah gets it right he says, "Correct."
Then he reads aloud the description of how to find the lateral area
of a pyramid. He points to the formula, which he had put on the
board before school, and reiterates it slowly, referencing each part
of the figure as he does so, "A equals height times base." Together
they solve the first problem. Then he says, "You need to use this
[formula] to figure out how many squares of roofing you need to
roof your house. If you can't figure it out, you'll have to go down

the road and ask your neighbor John how to do it. He was the best math student in his class." (Most of the students smile.) Then he gives the assignment, "For tomorrow, pages 378 and 379."

Seventh Grade [about 20 minutes]

Immediately, he walks over to the seventh-grade area directly in front of his desk and says, "All right, seventh, pages 127 and 128. Exchange your papers." The last student in each row brings the assignment up to the person in the front and the others hand theirs to the student sitting in the desk behind them. As with the eighth grade, he reads the answers off very quickly, and the students make an "X" beside any answer that is wrong. He says, "Page 127, number one, $13.50; number two, $26, . . . number ten, $585, 24%, and 6%, etc." The grading takes about one minute for two pages containing thirty-eight discrete answers. The teacher then returns to his desk, sits down, gets out his EZ-Grader, and says, "Thirty-eight answers—one wrong, 97%, two, 95%, three, 92%, four, 90%, five, 88%." His eyes move down to the seventh-grade math area of his grade book, and he calls out the first name. Again, the students know their order by this time and call out either the number wrong or the percent score, if they know it. This process takes only another several minutes. Then, he stands up, moves to the area between their rows of desks, and gives the assignment for tomorrow, "Page 129 is about profit and loss." As usual, he reads the instructions for the first problem aloud, verbatim, from the text, as the students follow along:

COMPUTING PROFITS ON THE SELLING PRICE

So far you have found the profit and the percent of profit on the cost. Many modern businessmen prefer to figure their profits on the selling price. Since commissions, discounts, and certain taxes are computed on the selling price, or total sales, it is simpler to compute the profits also on the sales. Furthermore, a merchant always knows what he receives for an article, but it is sometimes hard to separate the exact cost of the article from the operating expenses. Always state whether the percent of profit or loss is computed on the cost or on the selling price.

Exercises
1. Joe sells eggs at 40 cents a dozen. If his profit is 15% of the
selling price, how much does he make on 1 doz. eggs?
(Strayer-Upton,
Practical Arithmetics Book Three, 129)

The teacher looks at the pupils and says, "What would his profit
be if the eggs sell for forty cents a dozen?" Several hands go straight
up (no waving; no whispering for attention). He waits until a number of them have figured it out, and then calls out one girl's name,
"Susan?" She says, "Six cents," and he responds, "Exactly." Then he
says, "Just do 129 for tomorrow." The students go to work immediately, and he moves back to his desk to pick up the sixth-grade volume of this arithmetic series.

Sixth Grade [about 20 minutes]
The content changes; but the format (grade; take grades; introduce) and techniques (read instructions aloud; do a problem or
two) used for the sixth-grade math period are the same as that used
for each of the other two classes. He does spend a bit more time
here with process, since they have the least experience in his classroom. They are all accustomed to his method by this time though,
so the period goes very smoothly. The major difference from the
other two classes is that many of the sixth graders haven't yet
learned to trust their own scoring of someone else's paper, so they
ask many more questions about what is the right answer than do
the other two classes.

10:35
The teacher returns to his desk and works there, allowing time
for a few questions from students who come up to his desk. They
come up and stand quietly on either side of his chair; he answers
each question completely, and then turns to the next in line. The po-
liteness with which they do so is remarkable.

10:38–11:15   RECESS
At 10:38 he says, "Put your books away." He waits about ten seconds and says, "You're excused." The children get up; the noise

level increases dramatically as they go to the cloakroom to get their snacks (Barbeque corn chips; candy bars; licorice; Skittles, etc.). Most put on their coats, and head outdoors to play basketball or to sled. Some stay indoors and play Ping-Pong, read, or talk together or with their teacher.

At 11:10 he picks up his bell, walks to the back door and rings it there, then to the stairwell and rings it again. Then he returns to his desk and looks over the English assignment.

11:15–12:10   ENGLISH

All three grades use the appropriate workbook for *Climbing to Good English Six, Seven,* or *Eight.*

Eighth Grade [about 12 minutes]

The teacher begins by asking the students to keep their own workbooks because he doesn't intend to grade the assignment for today. The assignment had been to write some couplets and some limericks. Lesson 68 (Writing Short Verse) briefly discusses concepts of rhythm and rhyme, then defines the concepts *couplet* and *limerick.* On the previous school day, the teacher had quoted the definitions and examples directly from his annotated teacher's edition while the eighth-grade students read along with him from their workbooks:

The couplet consists of two lines of verse that rhyme. Both lines are the same length and rhythm. Together they make a complete thought. Capitalize each new line in poetry. Punctuate as you would any other sentences (no commas at ends of lines unless they are necessary).

Examples

Hear the stream go bubbling by
Like a gentle lullaby.
Why has not man a microscopic eye?
For this plain reason—man is not a fly.

A. Complete the following by adding a rhyming line. Remember to match the length and rhythm and to make a complete thought. You may also change the first line if you wish.

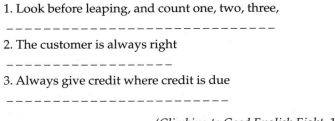

1. Look before leaping, and count one, two, three,

_____

2. The customer is always right

_____

3. Always give credit where credit is due

_____

(*Climbing to Good English Eight*, 149)

The day before, the teacher had also read aloud a description of the limerick, while the students followed in their text. As part of this day's work, the teacher spends ten minutes going around the class, moving from one student to the next in their seating order, asking them to read aloud their couplets and limericks. Most have an example of at least one form that they are willing to read aloud. Although there is occasional embarrassment, evidenced by blushing and a low voice, the teacher is very careful not to respond to the embarrassment. (In fact, I found him to be quite adept at avoiding that issue with these fourteen-year-olds.) Several who do not wish to read an answer simply shake their heads, and he goes on immediately to the next student. Then he asks them to read at home the final section of Lesson 68 that discusses and gives examples of the lyric poem. He also assigns Lesson 69, "Writing Longer Poems" (*Climbing to Good English Eight*, 150–155). Then he gives the written assignment: "Let's each write a poem four stanzas long. Choose a theme or ideal to discuss and then make a list of rhyme words that you might use. I'll give you until a week from Friday to finish it. Make it a nice poem, something to take home and cherish for years to come."

With no further words he proceeds directly to the assignment for the next lesson, "Lesson 70 is for tomorrow. It deals with conjunctions—I think you already know what these are." The lesson treats both coordinating and subordinating conjunctions, and constitutes a final review of a subject that was first introduced in grade five and has been practiced and reviewed several times each year since that grade.

Having assigned the work for the next day in the eighth grade, he returns to his desk, where he will spend five minutes answering questions on math from two sixth graders and seven eighth graders. We must remember that he has just finished teaching English to one class, and must still complete two more English lessons. His own thinking is headed in that direction. Now he will quickly shift gears and answer questions in a radically different subject area, posed by students from two different grade levels, in the order that they arrive at his desk. That he does so calmly, adequately, and will full attention to each of the students is a tribute not only to a gifted teacher, but also to a cultural perspective that values the *qualities* of life experiences and avoids frantic behavior. At 11:36, having answered the current set of questions, he walks to the seventh-grade area of the classroom.

Seventh Grade [about 12 minutes]

He begins immediately with Lesson 68, which mirrors that of the eighth grade. (You will recall that this unique series broaches the subject for two grade levels, i.e., teaming fifth with sixth, and seventh with eighth.) He spends about five minutes having them read aloud their couplets and limericks, admonishing them beforehand to speak loudly as they read their poems. When he introduces the long-range poetry writing assignment (the same as for the eighth grade), he reads aloud several of the longer poems in their text (Longfellow's *A Psalm of Life*, Saxe's *The Blind Men and the Elephant*, and an anonymous poem entitled *The Resurrection Power*). He reads with a strong voice, very rhythmically, pausing occasionally for emphasis. He counts the syllables for them in Longfellow's poem as he explains unaccented and accented syllables. He lists the rhyme words orally. And he also uses this poem to briefly discuss concepts of line and stanza, of mood, and of purpose. Much of this information is outlined for him in his excellent annotated text, but he presents the material in a delightfully winsome manner. With virtually no pause, he then proceeds to the immediate assignment for the next class session—Lesson 70 on conjunctions. He reads the textual explanation aloud to the seventh graders, since this is the first time they will have seen and heard it. The explanation covers one page in the text and takes several minutes to read aloud. Topics introduced with examples include coordinating and subordinating conjunctions, correlative conjunctions, and conjunctive adverbs (*Climbing to Good English Seven and Eight, Teacher's Annotated Edition*, 154). He gives particular emphasis to the *not only . . . but also* construction as a single conjunction separated by words which they link into one concept. He closes his introduction to this topic by saying, "It's very important to learn these because when you are writing a letter, it gets really boring for the reader if you use *and, and, and*. A new conjunction kind of decks it out. Learn to write to catch the person's attention." At 11:50, he turns his attention to the sixth grade.

Sixth Grade [about 12 minutes]

He tells them that they will grade Lesson 62 (review of pronouns and subject/verb agreement), starting on page 103. Then he walks over to the desk of an eighth grader who has had his hand in the air patiently for a minute or two. This consultation takes several minutes. When he finally returns to the sixth grade it is 11:53. He takes two minutes to grade their work, which includes seventy-seven discrete points. When he returns to his desk to take their grades, he finds three eighth graders waiting for him with math questions. This takes about two minutes. By 11:57, he is ready to take the English grades of the sixth graders. From 11:58 to 12:01 he answers questions from two sixth graders about grading, and one seventh grader, and two eighth graders about math.

During this interlude a number of children have taken foil-wrapped lunches over to the coal stove and placed them on a warming rack on its top.

By 12:01 he can return to the sixth-grade assignment, Lesson 64, on skimming and summarizing. He begins by reading aloud the directions on how to skim and to summarize:

> There are many different ways of reading. When we read for enjoyment or entertainment, we read slowly and leisurely. But when we look for information or search the paper for news, we

read quickly. This is called *skimming*. When we skim, we look over a page rapidly to see what it is about. We do not read every word or every sentence. It is important to learn how to skim for information.

When we tell about the main idea of what we read or heard, we are *summarizing*.

(*Climbing to Good English Five and Six*,
Teacher's Annotated Edition, 114)

Then he reads to them a paragraph that they are to summarize for their first assignment. The students read silently in their workbooks as he reads the paragraph aloud:

Indians were the first people to live in America. They made their homes in North and South America many years before Christopher Columbus reached the Western Hemisphere. Columbus called them Indians because he thought he had reached India. Some Indians lived simply. They fished and hunted animals in thick forests where modern cities now stand. Their canoes glided quietly along rivers now crowded with ships. Some Indians developed advanced civilizations. They created beautiful arts and crafts, invented calendars and systems of mathematics, and organized great empires. Indians lived in so many different ways that we cannot talk about "the typical Indian." The throbbing drums of the early Indians have grown silent, and their vast temples have fallen into ruins. But America's Indian heritage remains.

(*Climbing to Good English Five and Six*,
Teacher's Annotated Edition, 114)

The assignment involves two parts, the first of which is to answer four content questions about the paragraph, e.g.,

A. "Why were they called 'Indians'?" (114). The second part sends the students to the encyclopedias and dictionaries and other resources which every school has available in each classroom:

B. Find information about early American Indians in several different places, such as encyclopedias, social studies books, or other books from the library. Skim the articles about American Indians and write important information under each heading below.

(*Climbing to Good English Five and Six,*
Teacher's Annotated Edition, 114)

The three topics on which they are to gather information are: food, clothing, and shelter. The teacher reminds them what a summary is, "Basically, it tells the story in a short paragraph." He concludes the lesson by saying, "A good way that I was taught in [Amish] school was this. Usually the first line in every paragraph summarizes its content." At this point all eyes and ears in all three grades are fixed on him because this was anecdotal information from a respected member of the community about the past and its lessons.

By 12:07, the teacher has returned to his desk where he consults with three students, one from each grade. At the same time several sixth-grade boys go to the bookcase, get out a *World Book* volume, take it back to one of their desks, and look through it for information on American Indians. (This teacher deliberately encourages his students to work together in clusters of two or three because he believes that they will need this skill later in adult life. The students never attract his attention by noise or movement. Other teachers do not allow group work.)

At 12:09 the teacher says, "Put your books away." He waits a minute, and then says, "Let's bow our heads in prayer." Instantly the room becomes pin-drop silent as each person bows their head and prays silently.

12:10–1:30   NOON RECESS

After about a minute, the teacher looks up and says, "Anna," and her row of eighth graders gets up and goes to the cloakroom or to the stove to get their lunches. After thirty seconds he says, "Next row," and after a few seconds more, "Next," until all have been dismissed to get their lunches. The noise level rises dramatically as some of the students rush to the cloakroom. They also know that they can chat for the few minutes it takes before everyone is ready to eat. After they have gotten their lunches, they return to their own seats to eat without much talking. The teacher talks with several students who have come up to his desk while the others eat. (He pays attention to them while they eat since he can eat while they have their recess.)

By 12:25 he tells them, "You are dismissed." They leave in a great rush and with lots of noise—and even some shoving. Most will play outside (He encourages them to "run out and get some fresh air") to sled or play basketball (mostly boys) or to play "freeze tag" or "fox and geese" (mostly girls). A few girls prefer to stay indoors and chat for part of the time, but all leave for much of the time. The teacher eats his lunch, drinks some milk-coffee, and we chat for a while before he turns to his preparations for the afternoon period. (On other days, he goes outside to play basketball or volleyball with the children.)

A group of third-, fourth-, and fifth-grade boys comes looking for me to see if they can once again stump me with a test of my powers of observation. This time it's a question, posed by a third grader, "How long was the ark that Moses built?" I answer up semiconfidently, knowing that I'm destined to lose again anyway, and say, "Thirty cubits." At this they all laugh happily, and inform me that I wasn't paying attention. It was not *Moses* who built the ark.

At 1:25, the teacher rings his bell at the door and stairwell. He gives them five minutes to get to their seats—including a visit to the outhouse that lies just outside the school building. By 1:30, all have shed their coats, caps or bonnets, boots (some girls), and black gloves, and are seated quietly looking at him.

1:30–2:20   READING

All seven of the Amish parochial schools that I visited from January through May used the series of reading materials from Pathway Publishers, an Amish publishing group in Aylmer, Ontario, Canada and in LaGrange, Indiana.

Eighth Grade [about 15 minutes]

As usual, the work begins with a grading session. The eighth graders exchange their workbooks and grade the previous day's assignment that was the beginning of a new unit entitled "Nature's Wonders." Works assigned included a poem by Annie Johnson Flint entitled "The Creator;" another poem by Joseph Addison entitled "Spacious Firmament on High," and an essay on the stars entitled "Once in a Thousand Years" written by a Mennonite teacher. The reading assignment entailed twelve pages, nine of which were devoted to the essay. At the end of the essay was a list of words which the students were to study as part of their homework, knowing the definition and spelling of each: *embellish, preposterous, conjecture, lavish, faction, petrified, armistice, hoax, premature, and radial.* After each selection there is a section called "Thinking It Over", which the teacher had touched on in the previous class. One of the five activities or questions reads:

> Author Brackbill mentions Venus, Jupiter, Saturn, Sirius, The Milky Way, Arcturus, and some others. You won't need to wait a thousand years to see these. A good star book will help you locate them. Or perhaps you know someone in your neighborhood who is a star fan, who will be glad to spend an evening with you under the starry heavens. By the way, a flashlight is excellent for pointing out the stars.
>
> (*Our Heritage*, 297)

(This assignment had been given before the Hale-Bopp comet was visible. When it first became visible I was in a different Amish school, in their seventh- and eighth-grade classroom, where they eat lunch with virtually no talking at all. Suddenly, in the midst of the silent lunch, the teacher asked, "Did anyone see the comet last night? When I was finished choring, I came out of the barn, and there it was in the northwestern sky. It must have been around 8:30 or 9:00." He then showed us with his hand exactly where to find it; and that evening this professor had his first glimpse of a comet he didn't even know was present, so absorbed was he in his sabbatical leave project.)

The grading of the workbook takes only three minutes. The scores which the eighth graders report by percent are typical of their work: 97; 93; 100; 97; 97; 97; 93; 97; 97; 97; 90. The grading scale used by this teacher for his three grade levels is: A+=98; A=95; A-=92; B+=90; B=87; B-=84; C+=81; C=78; C-=76; D+=74; D=72: D-=70; and 69 or below is an F. The teacher then gets up and moves back to stand between his two rows of eighth graders to give the assignment for the next class. It includes William Cullen Bryant's poem "To a Waterfowl," two additional poems, and a brief piece on icebergs written in 1884 by the author of *Two Years Before the Mast*. Since he is somewhat pressed for time, he does not go over the study questions with them aloud. Instead, he makes an announcement for the following week, "Study from 7 through 240 for a semester test on Monday. It will be mostly words and meanings. I'll go across it with you for sure on Monday morning." He then goes back to his desk to get the seventh-grade workbook.

Seventh Grade [about 15 minutes]

When he is standing between the two rows of seventh graders, he says, "Seventh grade. We have five poems to grade, beginning with 'Service' [Edgar Guest]." The grading of their workbook pages takes about two or three minutes. After answering several quick grading questions with a simple, "No," or, "That's all right," he returns to his desk and takes down the grades, which range from 85% upwards, with most in the 92% area. He also takes their grades from the previous reading assignment since he hadn't had time to enter them in his grade book during that day's work. Instead of giving them a new reading assignment, he says, "Do that review for Unit 5, and study from 11 to 241 for the test on Monday. We're a little late on that (the first semester test)." He moves back to his desk and picks up the sixth-grade reader, since they had had no assignment to grade from the previous day.

Sixth Grade [about 20 minutes]

He stands at the front between the rows of sixth graders, and says, "Okay. Listen carefully. Let's read the three poems beginning with 'The Quest' on page 317." He starts at the front of the room and stands beside a student's desk, says the student's name, and that student reads the first stanza:

There once was a restless boy
Who dwelt in a home by the sea,
Where the water danced for joy
And the wind was glad and free;
But he said, "Good mother, oh! Let me go;
For the dullest place in the world, I know,
Is this little brown house,
This old brown house,
Under the apple-tree."

(Step By Step, 317)

As the boy finishes reading the first stanza, the teacher gets a happy and quizzical look on his face and says, "Oh! I remember that poem. It is about a boy who went searching for a better place to live . . . and found it at home, or something on that order. You read the poem and figure it out." Then he moves on to the next student, calls his name, and the student reads the next stanza. This process continues until the poem is finished. Then the teacher reads aloud the first question about the poem, "Where did the restless boy think was the dullest place in the world?" *(Step By Step*, 318) Most of the hands go up, and he nods at one who says, "Home." He nods again. Then they move on to the next (anonymous) poem entitled "A Mother's Love," which he reads aloud in its entirety in a strong expressive voice:

Her love is like an island
In life's ocean, vast and wide,
A peaceful, quiet shelter
From the wind, the rain, the tide.

'Tis bound on the North by Hope,
By Patience on the West,
By tender Counsel on the South
And on the East by Rest.

Above it like a beacon light
Shine Faith, and Truth, and Prayer;
And through the changing scenes of life
I find a haven there.

(Step By Step, 319)

When he finishes reading he speaks about a mother's love comforting us during the storms of life. Then he asks, "Does that mean thunderstorms, snow storms?" One of the sixth-grade girls holds up her hand. He nods at her, and she says, "the down points of life." He nods again. Then he says, "Study from 201 through 268 for the test Monday. Just review for Unit 7; that's all you have to do for Monday." By this point the busses have arrived, and so he returns to his desk where an eighth-grade girl is waiting with a question about the reading assignment.

2:20   BUSSES ARRIVE

2:25   DISMISSAL

He spends several minutes talking with the eighth grader about her question. Then he stands and walks over to the sixth-grade area and says something about their geography assignment, which is scheduled for the next day, "I want you to look up these rivers and see which way they flow: the Maumee, the Saint Mary's, and the Saint Joe." Then he looks over at the seventh grade and says, "Seventh grade. On number three on page 151 in your math, if we multiply by 195, you get a number that's way out of this world."

Then he says, as he always does at the end of the day, "Put your books away." He waits a moment, and then says, "Eighth," and after several more moments, "Seventh," and finally, "Sixth." The pupils get up quickly and go to the cloakroom and put on their wraps, while the teacher walks slowly to the back of the room, opens the door, holds it open and says a cheery, "Goodbye," or, "See you," to the children as they go out to the busses.

He returns to his desk; arranges a few things; picks up his thermos bottle; goes to the cloakroom to get his coat and his hat and his lunch cooler. He walks over to the coal stove and shakes it down and then adds a bucket of coal to hold it over until morning. He checks the damper; goes to several windows that have been opened slightly; closes them and pulls down the window shades to preserve the heat overnight. Then he walks with his own children over to the barn, hitches up the horse, and they leave for home, about a half mile away. By 2:45, the school sits empty of people and noise until the next morning.

Notes

Chapter One

1. I first saw this statement in an upper-grade history text in an Indiana Amish school.

2. Andrew Gulliford, *America's Country Schools* (Washington, D.C.: The Preservation Press, 1984), 35.

3. Donald B. Kraybill, *The Riddle of Amish Culture*, rev. ed. (Baltimore: The Johns Hopkins University Press, 2001), 21.

4. *Indiana Amish Directory of Elkhart and Lagrange Counties* (1980) n.p., 19.

5. *Amish Directory of the Nappanee, Kokomo and Milroy Communities* (1985) n.p., 28–29. We must assume that there were nine grades rather than eight because this predated the 1972 Supreme Court decision and one or more pupils had not reached the mandatory age for leaving school.

6. *Indiana Amish Directory of Elkhart, LaGrange, and Noble Counties* (1995) n.p., 13.

7. *Articles of Agreement Regarding the Indiana Amish Parochial Schools and Department of Public Instruction* (1967), Indianapolis, Indiana: Department of Public Instruction.

8. *Regulations and Guidelines for Amish Parochial Schools of Indiana* is available from the Gordonville Print Shop in Gordonville, Pennsylvania, 17529.

9. *Wisconsin v. Yoder et al.* 1972. United States Supreme Court. No. 70-110.

10. If the teacher is also a minister in the church, reading from religious materials is very acceptable, for they are ordained to a set-apart ministry; if the teacher is not a minister, then the usual approach is to sing religious songs with the pupils.

11. *Blackboard Bulletin* (January 2001), LaGrange, Indiana: Pathway Publishers, 24.

12. Ibid., 8–9.

13. Ibid.

14. *Amish Directory of the Nappanee, Kokomo and Milroy Communities* (1985) n.p., 28.

15. *Indiana Amish Directory of Elkhart and LaGrange Counties* (1980) n.p., 19–20.

16. *Amish Directory of the Nappanee, Kokomo and Milroy Communities* (1985) n.p., 29.

17. The Allen County Amish do not publish information about their schools. I am grateful to an anonymous Amish source (a significant figure in the Indiana Amish school movement) for this information.

18. *Blackboard Bulletin* (January 2001), LaGrange, Indiana: Pathway Publishers, 24.

19. *Indiana Amish Directory of Elkhart, LaGrange, and Noble Counties* (1995) n.p., 13.

20. *2002 Indiana School Directory*, Indiana Department of Education; and Corporation and School Snapshots (doe.state.in.us).

21. Ibid.

22. Ibid.

Chapter Two

1. For further definition of this concept see Hostetler, *Amish Society*, 4th ed.; Kraybill, *The Riddle of Amish Culture*; Harroff, "Sights and Sounds of the Amish Way," *Old Fort News* 44, no. 1 (1981), 1–13.

2. *Indiana Amish Directory of Elkhart and LaGrange Counties* (1980) n.p., 16.

3. *Blackboard Bulletin* (January 2001), LaGrange, Indiana: Pathway Publishers, 7.

4. I am indebted to Victoria Bridegam for this information contained in an unpublished paper.

5. This tabulation involves only the five largest settlements. It is based on data from the 2000-01 School Directory published in *Blackboard Bulletin* (January 2001), 7–24.

6. A fuller discussion of this question as it relates to the schools may be found in Harroff, "Value-Oriented Teaching in a Contemporary Indiana Amish Parochial School: Preparation for Adult Life through Faith, Responsible Behavior, and Community Interaction," *International Journal of Educational Reform* 7, no. 3 (July 1998), 243–254.

Chapter Three

1. The Ordnung of the various districts in the settlement in which the school is located determines such color choices. The color violet, for example, is not used in the Allen County settlement.

2. I am indebted to Kathleen Fuller for this information.

3. Hostetler and Huntington, as sociologists, discuss formal measures of personality type in their book *Children in Amish Society*, listed in the bibliography. I will focus on actual behaviors that I have observed over the years from Amish children in both parochial and public school settings, since I cannot speak to the theoretical issues.

Chapter Four

1. *Regulations and Guidelines for Amish Parochial Schools of Indiana* (1989 revision), pg. 5.

2. Robert Redfield, "The Folk Society," *American Journal of Sociology* 52 (January 1947), 293–308. See also the discussion by John Hostetler, *Amish Society*, 4th ed. (Baltimore: The Johns Hopkins University Press, 1993), 3–24.

3. During the 1997-1998 school year, I observed the work of one non-Amish teacher in an Amish parochial school. She is a well-known local person whose ancestry is Anabaptist, and thus she understands the belief and practice of her pupils very well.

4. The text in the Luther translation reads in German "*demütig sein vor deinem Gott.*" The text that I quote is the one used in the Indiana Amish schools for teaching German to upper grade pupils: *Special English-German Edition, The Holy Bible* (Grand Rapids: Dickinson Brothers Inc.), 1508–1509.

5. I should also add that I have worked with Amish carpenters, too, and I found my skills, my speed, and my endurance constantly tested and falling short. The Amish ability for sustained, high-energy work is an admirable quality.

6. My thanks to Kathleen Fuller for this observation from an unpublished paper.

7. We should also note that this is a general expectation among the Amish. Church officials (bishops, preachers, and deacons) work many hours each week at these jobs for no pay. They must do their own on-the-job training, consult with other ministers, preach, and otherwise heed their flock while also finding some way to have full-time income-producing work. It is a major responsibility, and only a preacher's family can really know how great the sacrifice is, and how few evenings are spent relaxing or even doing one's own work.

8. I do know two teachers who are married and who do not teach in their own church district. Each of them must travel about five miles to school—a distance that makes buggy travel difficult in bad weather, and very long. One of these teachers does drive his buggy to school. The other, who brings her children with her, hires a driver to bring her and pick her up every school day. Not only is this arrangement rather costly, it also causes her some anguish, since he sometimes drives into the school yard and honks his horn impatiently if she is not immediately ready to leave. Such loudness does not comport with the Amish understanding of modesty; such rudeness embarrassed me as a member of the surrounding "English" society.

9. The year before (1996), one of the most experienced Amish schoolteachers in the state had retired after nearly thirty years of teaching in one Amish parochial school. He was one of the early leaders in Amish parochial education in the state. He still substitutes today in his settlement.

10. *Blackboard Bulletin* (November 1999), LaGrange, Indiana: Pathway Publishers, 22. For purposes of my count I have not included two aides who are listed as "helpers."

11. Their home dialect of German is called Dietsch or Deitsch, depending on whether they use Swiss German or what they call "High German" at home. See Chad Thompson, "The Languages of the Amish of Allen County, Indiana:

Multilingualism and Convergence," *Anthropological Linguistics* 36, no. 1 (1994), 69–91.

12. We must remember that these are children whose first language is a dialect of German where the pronunciation rules are fixed and very regular in contradistinction to the vagaries of English pronunciation.

13. Nearly all Amish teachers use thought-provoking sayings like this in their classrooms. Other examples include: "People forget how fast you did a job, but they remember how well you did it," and "We can complain because rose bushes have thorns, or we can be thankful that thorn bushes have roses." I am especially indebted to Kathleen Fuller for these two examples.

Chapter Five

1. An example from the Elkhart-LaGrange settlement is a two-teacher school where one teacher works with grades one and two and with grades five and six; the other, with grades three and four and grades seven and eight. Using this division, each of these experienced teachers has sixteen pupils, has variety in her own preparations and grading, and yet the curriculum and textbook efficiencies of paired grade levels, particularly important in math and English, are maintained.

2. I am indebted to Victoria Bridegam for this information from an unpublished paper.

3. For this information I am grateful to an Amish bookseller in Indiana who wishes to remain anonymous.

4. *Learning more Numbers with Spunky*, 1.2 (Pennsylvania: Schoolaid, 1995), 75.

5. I am indebted to Amanda Stevens for this information.

6. I am indebted to Kathleen Fuller for this information.

7. For a detailed study written by a linguist who knows the Indiana Amish well, see Chad Thompson, "The Languages of the Amish of Allen County, Indiana: Multilingualism and Convergence," *Anthropological Linguistics* 36, no. 1 (1994), 69–91.

8. *Learning Through Sounds Book One* (Aylmer, Ontario: Pathway Publishers), frontispiece.

9. *Teacher's Edition: Learning Through Sounds Book One* and *Learning Through Sounds Book Two* (Aylmer, Ontario: Pathway Publishers), 115.

10. Ibid, page 116.

11. *Teacher's Manual for Learning Through Sounds* (Aylmer, Ontario: Pathway Publishers), 2.

12. *Teacher's Manual for Before We Read & First Steps* (Aylmer, Ontario: Pathway Publishers), 4.

13. Ibid., 40.

14. *Days Go By* and *More Days Go By* (Aylmer, Ontario: Pathway Publishers, 1975). (With relevant workbook and teacher's manual for both)

15. *More Days Go By* (Aylmer, Ontario: Pathway Publishers, 1975), 60.

16. Ibid., 64.

17. *Climbing Higher* (Aylmer, Ontario: Pathway Publishers), 242.

18. *Climbing to Good English Two* (Schoolaid, 1989), 158.

19. This series was used when I was in grade school in an Indiana public school during the early fifties.

20. The last page lists the name of the Zaner-Bloser Company in Columbus, Ohio.

Chapter Six

1. Elizabeth purchased these flash cards at a teacher's and homeschool supply store in Fort Wayne, Indiana. This very dedicated and gifted teacher enjoys regular outings to Fort Wayne to look at and purchase additional materials for her teaching.

2. Holey Cards (1978, n.p.) is a set of four cards available at Miller's Book Supply in LaGrange, Indiana.

3. Strayer-Upton, *Practical Arithmetics Book Three* (American Book Company: 1934), iii.

4. Judy Howe, *Arithmetic Four* (A Beka Book Publications: 1995), 4. This series was developed as a ministry of Pensacola Christian College (Florida).

5. Strayer-Upton, *Practical Arithmetics Book One* (American Book Company: 1934), 294.

6. I am indebted to Amanda Stevens for this information.

7. *Workbook for Building Our Lives* (Aylmer, Ontario: Pathway Publishers, 1985), 25.

8. Ibid., 26.

9. *Climbing to Good English Four* (Pennsylvania: Schoolaid), frontispiece.

10. Those of you who know Percheron workhorses know that their (usually) bobbed tails don't exactly catch much breeze.

11. Ibid., 131–133.

12. I am indebted to Kathleen Fuller for this information.

13. Theodore Kaltsounis, *The World and Its People: States and Regions* (Morristown: Silver Burdett, 1984). This is an excellent cultural geography/history text. The accompanying workbook includes much map work and exercises that support the content of the textbook. Such books, used for reading practice in class, also offer a wonderful contextual tool for strengthening the pupils' English reading skills

14. Ibid., 72–75.

15. At the time of its original printing it was developed for use in the American public schools, then revised for private schools and homeschooling.

16. Today we discourage this practice; but it has been used successfully since the dawn of bookmaking, by Benedictine priests in abbeys like St. Gall in Switzerland, where I have seen Latin texts with interlinear glosses in German.

17. Although I must say that the picture identifying *Mücken* on page 43 certainly looks like *Fliegen* to me.

18. This text was used by two of the schools that I visited; other health texts used for fourth grade include *Health*, published by Harcourt Brace Jovanovich, and *Health for All*.

Chapter Seven

1. In this regard, see Harroff, "Value-Oriented Teaching in a Contemporary Indiana Amish Parochial School," *International Journal of Educational Reform 7*, no. 3 (1998), particularly pages 249–251, where I discuss the question of responsible behavior.

2. Ibid., iv.

3. Ibid., 379. If you have decided to test your own math skills, the answers are 884,756 sq. ft. and 1106 da. (your answer is *wrong* if you did not use a label).

4. The Amish use this preposition rather than to say *go over* a topic.

5. Thank goodness I was on safer ground here.

6. This dual language edition of the Bible was photolithoprinted by Dickinson Brothers Inc. of Grand Rapids, Michigan. This edition is used in many Amish schools for upper-grade German.

7. I should hasten to add that a similar problem happens among younger Germans today in Germany. They no longer feel comfortable reading the older print style (*Fraktur*), and most younger people also prefer more "up to date" translations of the Bible in German.

8. After all, how many native speakers of English really know what *holpen* means? My word processor certainly doesn't; it just underlined it in red! In the time of King James, British English used that as the past participle of the verb "to help."

Chapter Eight

1. One must admit that some fine thinkers were produced in those one-room schools—Abraham Lincoln comes to mind.

2. Personal interview with author (March 1997).

3. In this regard, see my anecdotes about how teachers in Amish schools react when children misbehave during recess (Introduction and chapter three).

4. To the best of my knowledge, these grades are not reported to any state or Amish school authorities.

5. *Tips for Teachers* (Aylmer, Ontario: Pathway Publishers), 2.

6. Ibid., 3.

7. Ibid., 5. Even college German students enjoy testing their teacher occasionally. Thanks for the tip.

8. Ibid., 6. This, too, is a great summer break exercise for foreign language students. You don't grade their letters; you answer them.

9. Ibid.

10. Ibid., 8–9.

11. Ibid., 13.

12. Included among the games are directions for playing "Pom Pom Pull Away," the game of tag that was mentioned at the end of chapter four. And in the last chapter of *Tips for Teachers* the authors describe and give an address for ordering the EZ-Grader, which I have come to treasure for giving quick percentage grades on homework. I find it much easier to use than either my calculator or my computer spreadsheet.

13. Teacher's manual for *Days Go By* and *More Days Go By* (Aylmer, Ontario: Pathway Publishers, 1975), 2.

14. Ibid., 4.

15. Ibid., 4–5.

16. Ibid., 72.

17. Ibid., 3.

18. Ibid., 5.

19. Ibid., 3–4.

20. *Climbing to Good English Seven and Eight, Annotated Teacher's Edition* (Pennsylvania: Schoolaid, 1992), 33.

21. Ibid., 110.

22. Ibid., 112.

23. "From the Desk of Teacher Dave," *Blackboard Bulletin* (February 1999), LaGrange, Indiana: Pathway Publishers, 8. In this same column, Teacher Dave also recommends that teachers take one day per year to visit other schools so that they may pick up pointers from what other teachers are doing.

Chapter Nine

1. When I began my teaching career over thirty years ago, university and college campuses with dormitories stood in place of the parents for their students as well. When this practice changed during the sixties and seventies, the new approach brought with it a host of student behaviors that still plague college campuses.

2. In this regard see Stephen Harroff, "Value-Oriented Teaching in a Contemporary Indiana Amish Parochial School: Preparation for Adult Life through Faith, Responsible Behavior, and Community Interaction," *International Journal of Educational Reform* 7, no. 3 (July 1998), especially pages 249–251.

3. In the twenty or more years that I have observed Amish teachers in Indiana, I have not once seen a teacher resort to corporal punishment, although I have *heard* of it happening, from one person.

4. I must hasten to add that our faculty senate at the university has just as many rules about speaking out as does any Amish school, and senate officers to see to it that they are upheld.

5. It is increasingly easy for Amish teachers to find suitable materials. Their choice has been strengthened immeasurably by the work of Pathway Publishers, Schoolaid, and the Gordonville Print Shop, which serve primarily Old Order Amish and Mennonite schools. The homeschooling movement has also added to the breadth of choice here. Of particular help are the new materials in math from Beka Books.

Chapter Ten

1.This is not true of all schools certainly. During the summer months many schoolyards are used as pasturage for sheep or horses by the farmer on whose land the school is located.

2. A topic under discussion in Allen County, for example, is how schools might more effectively help their special education students. Since the Elkhart-LaGrange Amish schools implemented a program years ago, they are called on to explain their program.

3. During the summer of 1999, one such auction was held to benefit a family with a medical emergency, and several large farm fields were needed just to park the buggies of the thousands of people who attended.

4. I am indebted to Betty Simons for this information.

5. This noun shows their German language heritage. This is called an adjectival noun construction, and it is very typical in German (*das Wichtige* = what is important).

6. That day, I observed two teachers and over sixty pupils working together efficiently and effectively in a setting so crowded that the teachers could not move beyond a small square at each side of the front of the room. And each taught without "bothering" her colleague.

7. I am grateful to Victoria Bridegam for this anecdote from an unpublished paper.

8. See Harroff, "Value-Oriented Teaching in a Contemporary Indiana Amish School: Preparation for Adult Life through Faith, Responsible Behavior, and Community Interaction" *International Journal of Educational Reform* 7, no. 3 (July 1998), 243–254.

Conclusion

1. *Blackboard Bulletin* (November 1999), LaGrange, Indiana: Pathway Publishers, 7–9. This does not take into account that the settlement in Nappanee had opened three schools and Daviess County one new school in the previous year, 1998.

2. *Blackboard Bulletin* (November 1999), LaGrange, Indiana: Pathway Publishers, 22.

3. "Amish Schools," *Blackboard Bulletin* (November 1998), LaGrange, Indiana: Pathway Publishers, 21.

4. "Summary: Amish, " *Blackboard Bulletin* (January 2001), LaGrange, Indiana: Pathway Publishers, 24.

5. Ibid., 21.

6. Ibid., 24.

7. Workbooks for the Pathway series cost about $3.00 to $4.00 each; workbooks for the Beka math series are more expensive, between $6.00 and $8.00. The school purchases all hardbound texts, so there is no cost to the pupil. If the school uses the old Practical Arithmetics series, the only cost to pupils is paper. Other supplies are bought at discount stores and are like those that public school pupils need.

8. I am indebted to Kathleen Fuller for this information.

9. Early in her life, my mother substituted in an Amish parochial school south of Monroe in Adams County where my parents lived at the time. On her first day as a substitute, she began her day as she always had in the public schools with the Pledge of Allegiance to the flag. The next morning before school—that means before daybreak—the bishop and preachers made a visit. When they inquired why she had begun the school day this way, instead of with the Lord's Prayer that is always used, she laughed and said, "As a Brethren woman, I certainly should have known better." One can only imagine the animated dinner conversations between those school children and their parents after school that first day with Mrs. Harroff as a substitute.

10. John A. Hostetler, *Amish Society*, 4th ed. (Baltimore: Johns Hopkins University Press, 1993), 156.

Bibliography

Amish Society (General)

Bender, Sue. *Plain and Simple: A Woman's Journey to the Amish*. New York: Harper, 1989.

Enninger, Werner. "Coping with Modernity: Instrumentally and Symbolically, with a Glimpse at the Old Order Amish." *Brethren Life and Thought* 33 (Summer 1988): 154–170.

Hostetler, John A. *Amish Society*. 4th ed. Baltimore: Johns Hopkins University Press, 1993.

Kraybill, Donald B., ed. *The Amish and the State*. Baltimore: Johns Hopkins University Press, 1993.

Kraybill, Donald B., and Olshan, Marc A., eds. *The Amish Struggle with Modernity*. Hanover: University Press of New England, 1994.

Kraybill, Donald B. *The Riddle of Amish Culture*. rev. ed. Baltimore: Johns Hopkins University Press, 2001.

Luthy, David. "Amish Settlements Across America: 1991." *Family Life* (April 1992): 19–24.

Luthy, David. "Amish Settlements Across America: 1996." *Family Life* (May 1997): 20–24.

Nolt, Steven M. *A History of the Amish*. Intercourse, Pa.: Good Books, 1992.

Redekop, Calvin W., and Hostetler, John A. "The Plain People: An Interpretation." *Mennonite Quarterly Review* 55 (October 1977): 266–277.

Smucker, Mervin R. "How Amish Children View Themselves and Their Families: The Effectiveness of Amish Socialization." *Brethren Life and Thought* 33 (Summer 1988): 218–236.

Warner, James M., and Denlinger, Donald M. *The Gentle People: A Portrait of the Amish*. New York: Grossman, 1969.

Indiana Amish

Harroff, Stephen. "Plain People at Worship: Contemporary Preaching Practices of Two Groups of Plain People in Indiana (Old Order Amish and Old German Baptist Brethren)." *Brethren Life and Thought* 23 (1978): 210–224.

Harroff, Stephen. "Living the Set-Apart Life: Sights and Sounds of the Amish Way." *Old Fort News* 44, no. 1 (1981): 1–13.

Längin, Bernd G. *Plain and Amish: An Alternative to Modern Pessimism*. Scott-dale, Pa.: Herald Press, 1994.

Meyers, Thomas J. "Population Growth and Its Consequences in the Elkhart-Lagrange Old Order Amish Settlement." *Mennonite Quarterly Review* 65 (July 1991): 308–321.

Thompson, Chad. "The Languages of the Amish of Allen County, Indiana: Multilingualism and Convergence." *Anthropological Linguistics* 36, no.1 (1994): 69–91.

Amish Schools

Blackboard Bulletin. Aylmer, Ont.: Pathway Publishers, 1957.

Byler, Uria R. *School Bells Ringing: A Manual for Amish Teachers and Parents*. Aylmer, Ont.: Pathway Publishers, 1969.

Fisher, Sara E., and Stahl, Rachel K. *The Amish School*. Intercourse, Pa.: Good Books, 1986.

Harroff, Stephen. "Value-Oriented Teaching in a Contemporary Indiana Amish Parochial School: Preparation for Adult Life through Faith, Responsible Behavior, and Community Interaction." *International Journal of Educational Reform* 7, no. 3 (July 1998): 243–254.

Hostetler, John A., and Huntington, Gertrude Enders. *Amish Children: Education in the Family, School, and Community*. 2d ed. Fort Worth: Harcourt Brace Jo-vanovich, 1992.

Regulations and Guidelines for Amish Parochial Schools of Indiana. Gordonville, Pa.: Gordonville Print Shop, 1989.

Keim, Albert N., ed. *Compulsory Education and the Amish: The Right Not to be Modern*. Boston: Beacon Press, 1975.

Stoll, Joseph. *The Challenge of the Child*. Aylmer, Ont.: Pathway Publishing, 1967.

Stoll, Joseph. *Who Shall Educate Our Children?* Aylmer, Ont.: Pathway Publishing, 1965.

Wells, Richard D. *Articles of Agreement Regarding the Indiana Amish Parochial Schools and the Department of Public Instruction*. Indianapolis: Indiana Department of Public Instruction, 1967.

Wisconsin v. Yoder et al. United States Supreme Court. No. 70-110. Argued: December 8, 1971; decided: May 15, 1972.

One-room Country Schools and School Consolidation

Drury, David. L. *One-Room School Houses in Allen County*. 1967.

Gulliford, Andrew. *America's Country Schools*. Washington, D.C.: The Preservation Press, 1984.

Heynen, Jim. "Lessons from a One-Room School." *Better Homes and Gardens* (March 1998).

Index